CHAOS DAEMONS

D0521643

By Alessio Cavatore & Gav Thorpe

CONTENTS

Introduction 3

Eternal Glory to Chaos! 4
The Realm of Chaos 6
Daemonic Incursions 14
The Damnation of Toreus 20
Chaos and Mankind 23

Daemonic Forces 27
Bloodthirsters 28
Keepers of Secrets 29
Great Unclean Ones 30
Lords of Change 31
Bloodletters 32
Daemonettes 33
Plaguebearers 34
Pink Horrors 35
Flesh Hounds of Khorne 36
Fiends of Slaanesh 37
Beasts of Nurgle 38
Flamers of Tzeentch 39
Bloodcrushers 40
Seekers 41
Nurglings 42
Screamers 43
Soul Grinders 44
Daemon Princes 46
Furies of Chaos 46
Skarbrand 47
Ku'gath 48
Fateweaver 49
Skulltaker 50
The Masque 51

Epidemius 52
The Blue Scribes 53
The Changeling 54
Karanak 55

The Infernal Host 56
Greater Daemons 58
Bloodletters of Khorne 60
Daemonettes of Slaanesh 62
Plaguebearers of Nurgle 64
Daemons of Tzeentch 65
Bloodcrushers 66
Flesh Hounds 67
Fiends of Slaanesh 68
Beasts of Nurgle 69
Soul Grinders 70

Daemonic Gifts 73
Gifts of Chaos 73
Gifts of Khorne 74
Gifts of Tzeentch 74
Gifts of Slaanesh 75
Gifts of Nurgle 75
Daemonic Steeds 76
Marks of Chaos 76

Chaos Daemons Army List 77
HQ 78
Elites 82
Troops 84
Fast Attack 86
Heavy Support 87

Summary 88

INTRODUCTION

Welcome, puny mortal, to Codex: Chaos Daemons – your definitive guide to collecting, painting and playing with an army of Chaos Daemons in the Warhammer 40,000 tabletop wargame.

THE WARHAMMER 40,000 GAME

The Warhammer 40,000 rulebook contains the rules you need to fight battles with your Citadel miniatures in the war-torn universe of the 41st Millennium. Every army has its own Codex book that works with these rules and allows you to turn your collection of miniatures into an organised force, ready for battle. This particular Codex details everything you need to know about the Daemons of Chaos, and allows you to use these supernatural creatures in your games of Warhammer 40,000.

WHY COLLECT CHAOS DAEMONS?

An army of Daemons of Chaos is a unique and powerful force of supernatural creatures. Spawned as an incarnation of Mankind's worst nightmares from the alternative dimension known as the Warp, Daemons are the deadly servants of the four Great Powers of Chaos. Under the command of gigantic Greater Daemons and hellish Heralds, the unstoppable daemonic hordes tear apart all mortals that dare oppose them, feeding on their body and soul alike.

HOW THIS CODEX WORKS

This Codex is split into four main sections that deal with different aspects of the army:

Warpspace and Chaos: The first section introduces the Daemons and their part in the Warhammer 40,000 universe. It includes details on the four Greater Powers of Chaos: Khorne, Slaanesh, Nurgle and Tzeentch, on their bizarre and terrifying domains in the Realm of Chaos, on the pantheon of their Daemonic minions and on the history of their millennia-long struggle against the Imperium of Mankind.

Daemonic Forces: Each character, troop type and vehicle in the Chaos Daemons army is examined in this section. Firstly, you will find a full description of the unit, detailing its place within the army and in the Warhammer 40,000 universe as a whole. Secondly, you will find complete rules for the unit and details of any unique powers they possess.

The Infernal Host: This section contains photographs of the Citadel miniatures available for your Chaos Daemons army, gloriously painted by Games Workshop's famous 'Eavy Metal team. This section is an inspirational guide for painting your Daemons, and includes different colour schemes and painting techniques that will help you make a truly unique Daemonic force.

Daemonic Gifts: A list of additional powers and special abilities that allow you to customise your units and create the most powerful of Daemons.

Chaos Daemons Army List: The army list at the end of this Codex takes all of the units presented in the Forces of Chaos section and arranges them so that you can choose an army for your games of Warhammer 40,000. A force organisation chart categorises the units you can choose into HQ, Elites, Troops, Fast Attack and Heavy Support choices. Each unit type also has a points value to help you pit your force against an opponent's in a fair battle.

FIND OUT MORE

While Codex: Chaos Daemons contains everything you need to play a game with your army, there are always more tactics to use, different battles to fight and painting ideas to try out. Our monthly magazine White Dwarf contains articles about all aspects of the Warhammer 40,000 game and hobby, and you can also find articles specific to the Chaos Daemons on our website:

www.games-workshop.com

ETERNAL GLORY TO CHAOS!

Beyond the boundaries of physical space, unrestricted by time or causality, there is a plane utterly incomprehensible to mortal minds. It lies on the other side of dreams and nightmares, created without form or structure. It exists far outside imagination; an impossible abstraction made real only by metaphor. It is composed of love and hate, fear and hope, ambition and despair, and yet is an uncaring, emotionless void. It is constantly reborn but has never changed, eternally shifting though static. No natural, preternatural or supernatural sense can see, smell or hear it, except through illusory analogues that drive men insane. It is a place where gods thrive in constant war, fighting over the raw stuff of anti-creation that birthed them.

This is the Realm of Chaos.

The Lord of Battle, Khorne, snarls and roars, possessed of towering and immortal fury. Slaanesh, the Dark Prince, indulges every pleasure and whim, no matter how immoral or perverse. Great Nurgle, the Lord of Decay, labours endlessly to spread infection and pestilence, thriving on death and disease. Tzeentch, the bizarre and ever-changing Architect of Fate, spins everlasting plots and destinies, and weaves powerful sorceries to bind the future to his will.

These are the Gods of Chaos.

In this unknowable realm titanic hosts clash, locked together in a conflict that is as old as the universe and can never be won. Armies formed of nothing but thoughtless energy rage and scream, driven onwards by the whims of their creators.

Sometimes, just sometimes, the Realm of Chaos shatters its boundaries and spills into the realm of mortals. Nightmare and terror is unleashed upon the worlds of Man and alien alike, as armies of slavering fiends and cavorting warriors pour forth alongside regiments of blood-red soldiers and batteries of brazen war machines. While the skies burn with magical fire and rivers of blood drown ravaged cities, the hosts of the gods slaughter and maim all in their path, feeding upon the souls of their victims.

These are the Daemons of Chaos.

THE REALM OF CHAOS

Through the dreams and nightmares of mortals, the changing tides of the Warp are moulded into a fantastical landscape and populated with legendary beings. Timeless and ever-shifting, this psychic visionscape is known as the Realm of Chaos.

The Realm of Chaos, also known as the Warp, the Immaterium or Warpspace, is a dimension parallel to our own, a universe devoid of matter and life, without laws of time and space. It is a random, unstructured dimension of pure energy and unfocused consciousness. It is Chaos, unfettered by the limits of physics and undirected by intelligent purpose. Warpspace is Chaos, Chaos is Warpspace; the two are indivisible.

The Chaos Gods and their dominions are one; both are formed of the same Warp energy. As a Chaos God gathers energy it expands, its corresponding influence on the Warp around it broadens and its territory in the Realm of Chaos grows. No two visions of these realms are ever the same, but all are founded upon the same basic themes and feelings. As extensions of the gods, the appearances of these domains are formed upon the same emotions that created their masters: Khorne's realm is founded on anger and bloodletting; Slaanesh's realm is a paradise of damning temptations; Tzeentch's lands are kaleidoscopic constructs of pure magic; and

Nurgle's lands are a haven of death and regeneration. Though realm and god are as one, the Chaos Gods each have a form that embodies their personalities and dwells at the heart of their territories. Attended to by their Daemons, the Chaos Gods watch over their territories, seeking a disturbance in the pattern of the Warp that signals intrusion or opportunity.

CHAOS DAEMONS

The Chaos Gods are not alone in Warpspace. They have created servants – Daemons – who are not so closely bound to the Warp. They are separate from the flow of their universe, small pockets of self-contained energy, and do not change with it. Daemons are beings of a completely different nature to their masters, and are the most numerous creatures in the Warp. A Daemon is 'born' when a Chaos God gives up a little of its power to create a separate being. This power binds a collection of senses, thoughts and purposes together, giving a personality and consciousness that moves within the Warp. The Chaos power can reclaim the

power and independence it has given to its Daemon children at any time, thus ensuring their loyalty. It is only through the loss of this power that a Daemon can be truly destroyed, its mind dissolving into the whirls and currents of Warpspace.

Daemons have no physical presence within the Warp. The Realm of Chaos is anathema to matter of any kind and ships that navigate its depths do so by taking a skin or bubble of 'reality' with them when they enter. Instead of having a true physical shape, Daemons project a form conjured from the Warp's raw energy. The bizarre and inhuman appearances projected by Daemons indicate their presence, status and allegiance to a Chaos God. These insubstantial forms echo (or are echoed by) the shapes adopted by Daemons in real space, and the children of a Chaos Power will create and project similar forms.

As with the Chaos Gods and their realms, these forms come to reflect the emotions a Daemon is based upon and have been shaped by centuries of feeding on belief. In the real universe a Daemon's form is no more physical than it is in the Warp, though it may appear to be made of normal matter. In fact they are beings of Chaos, of magic given shape and depth. When manifested in the material universe, Daemons have particular invulnerabilities and weaknesses, as well as many strange powers derived from their Warp-born nature. Slaying a Daemon's physical projection does not kill a Daemon, only its presence in reality; its true Warp power remains unharmed.

When a Daemon is 'killed' in the material world, it is not truly destroyed but banished to the void. It must remain there to regain its strength, and is sometimes absorbed completely by its creator, or will eventually manifest itself again. Legend has it that a Daemon banished in this way cannot return for a thousand years and a day, though it is of course impossible to prove such a belief through study, and time is meaningless within the Warp. The slight to a 'slain' Daemon's pride is considerable, and the Daemon is forced to endure the mockery of its fellows until it can return to corporeal form and avenge itself. The most powerful Daemons will call upon any servants and tributary Lesser Daemons to help them achieve their revenge. If it has any allies it may call upon them for aid, though all Daemons are cautious of doing so for such favours must inevitably be returned, and no Daemon welcomes the dominion of another creature, mortal or daemonic.

THE GREAT GAME

The Realm of Chaos is not merely the home of the Dark Gods. It is also their battlefield, the arena for the Chaos Gods' great game of supremacy. The Chaos Gods are constantly at war with one another, vying for power amid the immaterial planes. Despite their myriad differences, the Great Gods of Chaos have the same goal: total domination. Such absolute power cannot be shared – especially amongst gods.

⟶ THE BIRTH OF SLAANESH ⟵

Slaanesh, the Dark Prince, was given life by the hubris and decadence of the ancient Eldar race. At the height of their power, as their empire reached its zenith, the Eldar became lost in their own heightened senses and consciousness. With highly advanced technology, the Eldar did not need to labour or wage war, and instead dedicated their lives to whatever idle pursuits took their fancy. Over several generations, this indolence grew and grew, while in the Immaterium a new Warp Power stirred. Created by this growing indulgence and excess, the first motes of Slaanesh began to coalesce.

The dormant Slaanesh fed upon the unchecked psyche of the Eldar, drawing on their lust and ambition, their artistry and pursuit of excellence. In turn, as Slaanesh grew, its nascent dreams trickled into the minds of the Eldar and fuelled their desires, pushing them ever onwards towards their approaching doom.

Eventually the Eldar civilisation devolved into little more than pleasure cults, wholly dedicated to every act of physical, mental and spiritual fulfilment. The Fall of the Eldar was signalled by the birth-scream of Slaanesh that flowed across the Warp, signalling the Prince of Pleasure's arrival in the Realm of Chaos. The psychic implosion caused by Slaanesh's arrival devoured the worlds at the heart of the Eldar civilisation, and such was its ferocity that it overwhelmed the barrier between the real and unreal, forming the massive permanent Warpstorm called the Eye of Terror.

Rampant and hungry, Slaanesh devoured the minds of the Eldar, and across the galaxy the race was almost wiped out. Only a relative few Eldar survived Slaanesh's birth-feast; the youngest who were least touched by the depravity of their race; and a handful of lucky individuals who somehow remained hidden from Slaanesh's hungry gaze. Most of these survivors have become sworn enemies of the Dark Prince, and yet a few of them have formed isolated cabals that still behave as their ancestors did, perversely following the way of excess.

That is how events are viewed from the chronology of the real universe; in the Warp, things are different. The Realm of Chaos has no true time, and events do not occur in a strict sequence of cause then effect. In essence, Slaanesh has always existed in the Warp, and yet has never existed.

With the ebb and flow of energy within the Warp, the power of a Chaos God expands and contracts, and his realm will shift accordingly. For long periods one god may dominate the others, fed by its own success, leeching its foes' energy for its own growth. Ultimately, the other gods will ally against the dominant force and through combined efforts reduce him in power, until another of their number rises to prominence. This pattern is played out again and again through eternity. No Chaos God can ever truly be victorious, for if all other Warp Powers were obliterated, the Warp would become a still, unmoving mass and Chaos would no longer exist.

When the gods war, the Immaterium trembles and Warpstorms billow across the galaxy. Within the Realm of Chaos, hordes of Daemons are sent forth to do their master's bidding and the lands of the gods strain and heave at each other in physical assault. Possessed of personality and intelligence, the Daemons of a Chaos God aspire to draw favour – Warp energy – from their master, and often launch attacks of their own into the lands of rival Daemons.

Khorne's Daemons advance as a great legion, accompanied by blaring horns, beneath brazen banners, the whips of the Bloodthirsters urging on rank upon rank of vicious Bloodletters. With raw anger and violence, the legions of Khorne cut a swathe through enemy territory, the blood spilt by their attacks polluting the realm of the enemy, turning it into Khorne's wasteland.

When Nurgle's minions are set free, they march forth to spread disease and decay. Sonorous chanting and the rusted clangs of a thousand bells herald their attacks, while the army advances under an impenetrable swarm of flies. The noxious poxes and pestilence of the Great Unclean Ones kill everything in their path, rendering it down to a mulch from which evil-smelling fungi and plants erupt.

Slaanesh attacks in a more insidious manner, as might be expected. The first assaults are subtle, unnoticeable to the other gods. Inside the fabric of another god's realm, the tendrils of Slaanesh's power inveigle their way into root, bone and crystal, corrupting them from within. As the land itself becomes perverted to Slaanesh's power, it dulls the senses of the enemy's Daemons, allowing the fast-moving armies of Slaanesh to strike swiftly and decisively.

Tzeentch is perhaps the most dangerous of all the gods, for he will always create a weakness to exploit before attacking. Through plotting, innuendo and magic, Tzeentch frequently sets the other gods to war with each other. He waits patiently to see how these conflicts progress and when the time is right, his Pink Horrors and Lords of Change sweep forward upon a carpet of magic, striking at the weakest of the contenders. With magical blasts and warping power, the armies of Tzeentch quickly overcome all opposition, and newly claimed territory swiftly becomes part of Tzeentch's crystalline domain.

For the most part, at least one god will be contending with the others and this occupies the attention of all, drawing their gaze away from the mortal realm. It is not unknown though for all four of the gods to agree on a common purpose, although each only consents to such truces in order to gain some kind of advantage. Once in every few thousand years, as we reckon it, there arises a being, place or object in the material universe that attracts the attention of all the Gods of Chaos. So important is this new element, so desired or so dangerous, that all rivalry is temporarily put aside in order for Chaos to take advantage or thwart the threat. Then the Four work as one for a while, but as soon as their objective is achieved, the eternal struggle resumes.

For Mankind, the most significant occasion of this type was the rise of the Emperor. During this period the Chaos Gods tried with all their might to bring about the Master of Mankind's downfall, culminating in their corruption of the Primarchs and the wars of the Horus Heresy. Other events have led to brief cessations of conflict in the Realm of Chaos: particularly promising Black Crusades by Daemon Princes or Chaos Space Marine warlords; the extermination or birth of a new race; the rise of a new being. Such interest in mortal affairs is fleeting at best, and treaties between the gods do not last long. One god or another, or all four, eventually oversteps the bounds of the agreement and attempts to usurp his fellow gods. Once again the Realm of Chaos thunders to the march of armies and the roar of clashing gods.

THE FORMLESS WASTES

The Warp has no physical dimensions, and the Realm of Chaos is without limits or true geography. The areas of influence controlled by the Chaos Gods form their realms, and the rest of this roiling landscape is often referred to as the Formless Wastes, the Land of Lost Souls or the Chaos Abyss.

Much of the Formless Wastes is random chaos, constantly churning and reforming depending upon the whims of mortals and currents in the Warp. Here rivers of tar flow through petrified woodlands under crimson skies; great stairways lead into the heavens and join themselves from below in an ever-lasting loop; castles made of bones and fortresses of ichor stand amidst copses of limbs, and Pillars of fluorescent fire burn on the horizon. Every dream and nightmare, every lunatic vision and deranged fancy finds its home in the Formless Wastes.

The Formless Wastes are home to the Furies – Daemons created by indecision and random chance, fed by baseless fear and dread. In great flocks they circle through the actinic sky, searching for vulnerable, easy prey – the fluttering souls of mortals that have not yet been absorbed by the Warp. These weak apparitions appear as flickering spirits and disembodied voices, lacking anything but the most rudimentary awareness and instinct. The Furies sweep down upon these hapless beings and devour them, before scattering in fear at the approach of more powerful Daemons seeking the energy of the soul swarms.

It is also in the Formless Wastes that other powers create their abodes – the provinces of Greater Daemons and Daemon Princes grown powerful enough to instil a small measure of control over their surroundings. Small islands of structure sprout from the haphazard wilderness, some appearing for only an instant, others almost as old as the Great Powers. Each is a petty domain in comparison to the vast realms of the Chaos Gods, but each embodies the whimsy of its creator, a small shrine or temple to a niche of belief. These might even be populated by their own short-lived Daemons, though most fall prey to the Furies.

THE FORTRESS OF KHORNE

The dominion of Khorne is a monument to fury and bloodshed. It is built upon foundations of murder and conflict, and is home to every facet of battle and conquest. This blood-soaked realm echoes constantly with Khorne's bellows and the clash of weapons, the cracking of whips and the clarion calls of innumerable brass war-horns.

Khorne is the Blood God, Lord of War, Taker of Skulls. He is wrath incarnate, filled with a never-ending lust to dominate and destroy, to conquer and kill. The Blood God is broad and muscular, with the face of a savage, snarling dog. Khorne wears heavy, overlapping plates of armour fashioned from brass and blackened iron. His every word is a growl of endless fury and these roars of ire echo out across his land. Upon a throne of brass, Khorne sits atop a mountainous dais made of the skulls of his champions and their defeated opponents. Beside him rests a great two-handed sword, capable of laying waste to worlds with a single blow. This fell blade is known by various names, including Woebringer, Warmaker, the End of all Things and Bloodfeeder.

Khorne's gloomy chamber is lit by a great fire pit, where dark flames consume the souls of cowards who fled from battle. This haze-filled throne room sits in the central keep of the Brass Citadel, the castle of Khorne. Decorated with red-veined marble, the metal walls of this unholy citadel are broken by jagged outcrops, encrusted with blood and armoured with spurs of bloodstained brass. Hideous gargoyles leer from every parapet, ready to spew scalding streams of fiery metal upon a besieger. The moat of the Brass Citadel is filled not with water, but with the boiling blood of those who have lost their lives to war.

Beyond this moat lies league upon league of cracked land, littered with the splintered bones of those fallen in battle. Packs of Flesh Hounds prowl these wastes for intruders, skirting along the edges of seas of blood, roving through mazes of cracked bones, tracking down any interloper. The Flesh Hounds can catch the faintest scent of Khorne's foes even through the omnipresent stench of blood, and are merciless once on the chase.

This blasted wasteland is split by a great crevasse, a canyon many miles long and bottomless. It is said that Khorne himself was once consumed by such a rage that he took up his sword and smote the ground, splitting it asunder for eternity. Occasionally the Canyon of Death

fills with a tide of blood, which spills out over the plains and sweeps away the heaps of headless corpses and mountains of shattered bones in a tsunami of crimson, as if the universe bled from some hideous wound.

A chain of immense volcanoes, constantly smouldering, girdles Khorne's domain. These form the Ring of Doom. Khorne's roars of rage cause the volcanoes to erupt and the ground to shudder. The volcanoes then explode with the wrath of the Blood God, spilling out rivers of lava as hot as Khorne's anger. On the inward slopes of these jagged, fire-tipped peaks sprawl the foundries of Khorne. It is said that within these dire forges labour the souls of warriors who died in their sleep, forever doomed to serve Khorne as slaves. Great stacks billow forth clouds of smoke, which mix with the fumes of the volcanoes to choke the blood red skies with the industry of war. These grim edifices keep Khorne's armouries filled; his numberless warriors armed and armoured by ceaseless toil.

Here too can be found the pens of the Juggernauts. Behind buckled and cracked walls thicker than any mortal fortification, the Juggernauts of Khorne are corralled. Such a godly stockade is needed, for no lesser barrier could hold at bay the fury of these daemonic monsters. The titanic Juggernauts constantly fight amongst themselves, butting heads and goring each other to establish dominance. Legends tell of Daemons, and mortal Champions that Khorne has brought to his

realm, and who have dared the wrath of the Juggers to take a mount for themselves. The smashed remains of nearly all of these warriors are left smeared over the walls, only a few of the bravest and strongest have ridden from the great brass gates atop the back of one of these murderous beasts.

On the outward slopes of the volcanoes are immense parapets and bastions. Carved from black granite, these tower miles into the sky, a daunting defence against any unwise enough to assail the kingdom of the Blood God. Great infernal cannons await the command of Khorne to unleash the fires of battle on the realms of the other gods. Mighty fortresses guard the brass battlements of the Ring of Doom, packed with Khorne's bloodthirsty legions. With a single growl from Khorne these armies spill forth across the domains of the other gods to bring slaughter and battle. Under Khorne's urgings, his endless tide of soldiers are whipped into a blood frenzy, and will fall upon each other in their desire to spill blood if no other foe can be found.

For it is war – constant, mindless bloodletting and destruction – that is all Khorne cares for. He cares not who is victorious and who is slain, just that they fight until they can fight no more. All that Khorne exists for, all that his entire being is bent towards, is the flow of blood from fresh wounds and the taking of skulls.

THE PALACE OF SLAANESH

Few gods welcome intruders to their empire, but there is one who loves to tempt visitors to his unnatural domain. This is Slaanesh, the Dark Prince and Lord of Pleasure. Those that dare his realm risk becoming trapped in its warped delights for eternity. The Dark Prince's realm is divided into six domains, arranged in concentric rings about the Palace of Pleasure. Slaanesh's domain might be mistaken for a paradise, but nothing here is as it seems. Each region is not only a celebration of Slaanesh's desires, but also his chief defence. An intruder can only reach the Palace of Pleasure in the very heart of Slaanesh's territory by passing through all six of the circles – an act of will beyond most souls, both mortal and daemonic.

The circle of Avidity forms the outermost boundary of Slaanesh's domain. The temptations within its borders play upon an interloper's greed. Gold is found here in abundance, glittering ingots and coins beyond counting. Any who attempt to take this wealth are doomed to spend eternity counting and polishing their hoard. The circle of Avidity is divided by tall marble walls studded with gems of every colour of the rainbow. These jewels are the lairs of daemonic spirits that invade any wanderer who touches them, devouring his soul and destroying his body from within. At every corner and crossroads stand gilded statues, some of beautiful Slaanesh, others of Daemons and mortals trapped in blissful ecstasy. A trespasser who lays even the slightest touch upon these golden statues will join them, turning to gold while his soul remains trapped within his immobilised form.

Should greed not ensnare the unwary, the next circle is Gluttony. Here is a vast lake of wine, dotted with islands linked by criss-crossing bridges. On each island is a table creaking under a lavish banquet, each more delectable than the last. A single taste of the smallest morsel, a simple sip from the lake, entraps the soul, filling it with a hunger even the most sumptuous feast cannot sate. Eventually the intruder gorges himself so much that his bloated body simply expires from the strain, or explodes in a shower of gore and half-digested food.

Beyond lies the circle of Carnality, a debauched place where all manner of fleshly pleasures may be sampled. Lissom maidens and beautiful youths glide across verdant fields, their faces and fertile forms moulded to the perfect desire of the heart. Yet to engage with such a creature is utter folly, for the pleasing appearances of these lovers are simply glamours cast by the vicious Daemonettes of Slaanesh, who will tear apart any who lay a hand upon them.

Upon entering the next circle, the traveller is greeted by roars of adulation. This is the circle of Paramountcy, where intruders are tempted with power over others. For the visitor with martial ambition, an army so vast its number is beyond counting awaits upon an endless plain, in fevered anticipation of his commands for conquest. To the politically minded, this circle appears as a great chamber of debating and governance, from which he can rule entire worlds and command the respect of their populations. In this place of personal aggrandisement every whim is obeyed, every command fulfilled. Yet to linger within this circle is to eventually succumb to eternal, nagging paranoia; to see contempt beneath every smiling face and hear conspiracy in every obsequious response. Surrounded by the adoring throng, the visitor's own self-doubts become a tortuous prison from which there is no escape.

The circle of Vainglory is a mesmerising garden, its maze of paths thick with beautiful flowers and heavy with thorns. The gentle, fragrant breeze whispers of past glories, reminders of achievements great and small. Still, mirrored pools reflect the visitor as he sees himself, presenting him with the ideal self-image. Hubris is the snare in this domain, for each step an intruder takes whilst feeling boastful pride leads him further from the true path. As his pride swells, he is drawn into the depths of the wild garden and eventually becomes entangled in the choking undergrowth. The braggadocio swiftly falls prey to thorns whose pricks sting for all time, whilst around him the devil-dryads laugh scornfully, turning his glorious deeds into an ironic eulogy.

The last circle is the most perilous, after all of the ordeals already faced. It is the serene domain of Indolency; a never-ending beach where heavenly choirs sing soothing lullabies and the perfumed sea dulls the mind. The warmth of a summer sun calms the soul and the gentle washing of the lapping tide stills the heart. The white sands underfoot are the desiccated husks of those who have come before; to rest for even a moment is to fall into a coma, in which the traveller will die, content to waste away in idle bliss. If the visitor traverses this final and most insidious of circles he comes before almighty Slaanesh.

Of all the Chaos Gods, Slaanesh alone is divinely glamorous: long-limbed and elegant, with a haunting androgynous beauty. Some say that Slaanesh can assume male, female or hermaphrodite form at will. He usually manifests himself as a young man – clean limbed and fresh with the vigour of youth. Indeed, Slaanesh is seductive as only an immortal can be, disarming in his innocence, utterly beguiling in his manner. Some say that it is impossible for mortals to look upon that divine face without losing their soul, for all who see it become willing slaves to every whim of the Dark Prince, embracing his ways with wild abandon.

THE MAZE OF TZEENTCH

Tzeentch is the God of Change and the Master of Sorcery. His realm is woven from the raw fabric of magic, threaded upon deceit and conspiracy. Of all the outlandish landscapes of the Realm of Chaos, Tzeentch's domain is the most bizarre and incomprehensible.

The Crystal Labyrinth of Tzeentch sits upon an immense iridescent plateau; its presence is felt across all of the Daemonic realms. Interchanging, shifting avenues made of crystals of every colour criss-cross Tzeentch's realm. Hidden pathways built from lies and schemes infiltrate the dominions of the other gods, binding together the fractious Realms of Chaos.

The Crystal Labyrinth has no Daemonic warriors. Its own illusory causeways and passages are enough of a barrier to any intruder not possessed of the strongest mind imaginable. Its glittering corridors reflect not only light, but also hope, misery, dreams and nightmares. The Crystal Labyrinth does not merely reflect but also distorts, pulling apart aspiration and purpose, turning them to insanity and despair. Driven by Tzeentch's unconscious schemes, the Crystal Labyrinth constantly moves and rearranges; each curve and turn and dead-end is a passing whim of the Lord of Fate. Those lost within the maze's reaches will wander for eternity, their minds shattered, their dreams broken upon the wheel of their own failed ambition.

At the centre of the maze, hidden from those who have not the insane insight to find it, stands the majestic Impossible Fortress. Twisted crystal spires and towers of blue and pink flame writhe and burst from the fortress' core. These exist for only a heartbeat, then shimmer and disappear, to be replaced by new and ever more maddening architecture. Gates, windows and beckoning doorways yawn open like hungry mouths before shutting moments later, barring all access.

The nature of the Realm of Chaos is encapsulated within the Impossible Fortress. Physical space and time do not exist here. One might wander for weeks inside a chamber no larger than a thimble, or traverse leagues with a single step. Gravity shifts and changes, or disappears altogether. Light of every colour of the spectrum, and of shades unknown in the real universe, springs forth from the shifting walls.

For mortals, the mutating citadel is utterly impenetrable. So locked in their physical ways, men are driven insane, while their bodies might implode or be pulled apart by the forces unleashed by Tzeentch's meandering thoughts. Even Daemons cannot easily endure the twisted horror of the Impossible Fortress and only the Lords of Change can safely navigate its corridors. These, the Greater Daemons of Tzeentch, can tread the secret paths that lead to the inner sanctum within the Impossible Fortress; the Hidden Library where Tzeentch concocts his eternal plots.

The Hidden Library itself contains every scrap of knowledge, every thought of every creature across space and time. The books, parchments and scrolls are bound with chains of magical fire; row upon row, shelf upon shelf of all knowledge stretching into the infinite recesses of Tzeentch's lair. Trapped within the shifting labyrinth of the Impossible Fortress, countless Pink Horrors and Blue Horrors creep and crawl over the library, tending to the books as a mad gardener might tend to a sprawling mess of weeds and thorns. The grimoires chatter to their keepers, using their voices to trap the Horrors in webs of deceit and scandal so that the Daemons eventually fade away and the Hidden Library absorbs their energy.

Tzeentch is the most bizarre of the Chaos Gods. His skin crawls with constantly changing faces that leer and mock those who dare look upon him. As Tzeentch speaks, these faces repeat his words with subtle differences of intonation, providing a mocking commentary that casts doubt upon the original words. Tzeentch's puckered face is formed from his torso, so that head and body are one. From above Tzeentch's burning eyes spring two sweeping horns, the spiralling extremities of which crackle with arcane fire.

Tzeentch is the Changer of the Ways, the Great Conspirator – the Architect of Fate for the universe. He takes great delight in the plotting and politicking of others, and favours the cunning over the strong, the manipulative over the violent. None of Tzeentch's cogitations are simple, and indeed are often contradictory, for he aspires to nothing except eternal trickery and artifice.

In Tzeentch's eyes, mortal creatures are immeasurably steeped in deceit and ambiguity; yet somehow pass their daily lives completely unaware of the countless contradictions and blemishes in their souls. Tzeentch cannot help but to dabble in the mortal realm, sometimes as part of the Great Game against his brother gods, more often to satisfy his own need to meddle, manipulate and control. Tzeentch is not above sullying his hands with the clamour of war, though he much prefers to win battles through guile and devastating sorcery than brute force.

Trapped within his own ineffable thoughts Tzeentch has no goals or aims other than the weaving of complex schemes. While one mortal lies, while envy and ambition survive, Tzeentch will work his magic as the puppet master of the universe.

THE GUARDIAN OF THE MAZE

Within the convoluted labyrinth of Tzeentch, it is said there is one true path to infinite knowledge that any creature, mortal or daemonic, can follow. This road leads through nine gates, each barred against entry. The gates appear as golden arches thrice the height of a man, wreathed with purple, blue and pink fire. At each gate stands the Guardian of the maze, little more than a giant floating mouth in appearance. The nature of the Guardian is such that it stands watch over all nine gates at the same time.

When someone approaches one of the gates, the Guardian poses them a question, one of the Nine Hundred and Ninety-nine Riddles of Tzaratxoth. The Guardian itself has no ears and can never hear the reply, and so can never tell the secret to anyone, but the enchantment of the gates means they will open on the correct reply. The riddles are said to be so taxing that only the greatest lateral and logical thinkers can discern their answer. The Guardian swallows whole those intruders that give an incorrect response!

Legends tell that only one challenger, clad in the guise of a young girl with a little black dog, managed to make her way through all of the gates. When Tzeentch questioned him about this failure, the Guardian accused her of cheating.

THE GARDEN OF NURGLE

While the mortal realm is laid waste by blight and pestilence, the lands of Nurgle thrive on disease and corruption. Tended by the Lord of Decay, this unwholesome realm is home to every pox and affliction imaginable and is foetid with the stench of rot.

In death there is life. Upon the decay of the living thrive untold numbers of bacteria, viruses, insects and other carrion-feeders. All life feeds upon other life to exist, and from every plague grow new generations, stronger and more virile than before. As regeneration comes from decay, so hope springs from despair. The greatest inspiration comes in the darkest moments; in times of crisis are mortals truly tested and driven to excel. This is the creed of Nurgle, the Lord of Decay, Master of Pestilence. Though utterly foul to look upon, and creator of every infection and epidemic to have ever swept the universe, Nurgle is a vibrant god of life and laughter, not a morose purveyor of despair and gloom. As the god, so too his immortal realm. The domain of Nurgle is not a barren wasteland, but a macabre paradise of death and pestilence.

Under a sky thick with buzzing swarms of black, furry flies grows the Garden of Nurgle. Twisted, rotten boughs entangled with grasping vines cover the mouldering ground, beneath an insect-ravaged canopy of leaves. Fungi both plain and spectacular break through the leaf-strewn mulch of the forest floor, puffing out clouds of choking spores. The stems of half-Daemonic plants wave of their own accord, unstirred by the still, pungent air. Bright sprays of red, blue, yellow and purple puncture the gloom; havens of cheeriness in a dismal woodscape. Burrowing and scuttling beetles of all kinds, with brightly-patterned caparaces and shining wings, flit along the banks of sluggish, muddy rivers. Reeds rattle, whispering the names of the poxes inflicted upon the worlds of mortals by Great Nurgle; or lamenting those that have died from the fatal caress of their creator.

Jutting from amidst this primordial mire is Nurgle's manse. Decrepit and ancient, yet eternally strong at its foundations, the mansion is an eclectic structure of rotted timbers and broken walls, overgrown with crawling poison ivy and thick mosses. Cracked windows and crumbling stone compete with verdigris-coated bronze, rusted ironwork and lichen-covered cornices to outdo each other with their corrupted charm.

Within these tumbling walls, Nurgle toils. His gigantic body is bloated with corruption and exudes an overpowering stench. His skin is greenish, leathery and necrotic, its surface abundant with running sores, swelling boils and fruitful infestation. Nurgle's gurgling and pulsating organs are rank with the excrement of decay, spilling through his ruptured skin to hang like obscene fruit around his girth. From these organs burst swarms of tiny Nurglings that chew on Grandfather Nurgle's rotting bowels and suck upon his bountiful, nauseous juices.

Beneath mildewed and sagging beams, the great god works for eternity at a rusted cauldron, a receptacle vast enough to contain all the oceans of all the worlds of the galaxy. Chuckling and murmuring to himself, Nurgle labours to create contagion and pestilence – the most perfect, unfettered forms of life. With every stir of Nurgle's maggot-ridden ladle, a dozen fresh diseases flourish and are scattered through the universes to bring low civilisations and destroy the populations of worlds. From time to time Nurgle ceases his stirring, and reaches down with a clawed hand to scoop a portion of the ghastly mixture into his cavernous mouth to taste the fruits of his labour.

Dwarfed by their mighty lord, a host of Plaguebearers are gathered about Nurgle. Each chants sonorously: keeping count of the diseases created; of the Nurglings that have hatched; of the souls claimed by the Lords of Decay's putrid blessings. This hum drowns out the creaking of the rotten floor and the scrape of ladle on cauldron, so eternal in its monotony that to hear it is to invite madness.

When Nurgle's power waxes, his garden blooms with death's heads and filth, encroaching upon the lands of the other gods. War follows as Nurgle's adversaries fight back and the Plaguebearers take up arms to defend the morbid forest. From such war springs the richness of life and death, of triumph over adversity. Though Nurgle's realm will eventually recede again, it will have fed deeply on the immaterial bodies of those who have perished, and will lie in gestate peace for another eternity until it is ready to swell once more.

DAEMONIC INCURSIONS

The fantastical domains of the gods are populated with creatures as equally bizarre as their surroundings. These Daemons are a great threat to the galaxy, for unlike their masters they are not wholly confined to the Realm of Chaos.

Daemons are the agents of their god within and beyond his realm. Untold numbers of entities make up the daemonic host of each god. These legions consist of Greater Daemons, Daemon Princes, Lesser Daemons, Daemonic Beasts and other creatures beyond classification. Spawned and destroyed by the needs and whims of their Chaos God, the size of a god's forces swells and ebbs with the power of their master. Though often preoccupied by the Great Game of their creators, the Daemons of Chaos lust after the mortal realm. It is here that the Daemons can dominate and destroy, conquer and corrupt, in a material universe that can be permanently changed. For this reason, Daemons are constantly seeking egress into the realm of mortals where they can wreak havoc and increase the power of their master and gain worshippers of their own.

For most of their existence, Daemon armies war against each other and amongst themselves, depending upon the prevailing conflicts and alliances of the Dark Powers. The complexities of the gods' wars are such that

sometimes these armies will fight alongside the hosts of other gods against Daemons of their own kind. Khorne's warrior-Daemons fight against any enemy, for it is not victory but the slaughter that sustains them. The Daemons of Tzeentch often plot and conspire against each other, and it is common for them to aid the enemies of rival Tzeentchian Daemons. The thrill of battle entices Slaaneshi Daemons to fight without the bidding of their master, revelling in the sensuous excess of conflict. The Daemons of Nurgle feed upon the destruction of the realms of the other gods and will frequently join forces against other Nurgle Daemons to perpetuate an ongoing war, bringing about even greater decay and ruin. All of this means that at any given time, a Daemon army may contain creatures created by one, several or all of the gods, and it will fight against any and all opposition. Such is the nature of Chaos.

For the most part, the Chaos Gods care nothing for the affairs of mortals. They are only concerned with the eternal flow of emotion across aeons. Each mortal life is such a brief flicker in the long existence of Chaos that they barely register on the consciousness of a Ruinous Power, if they register at all. Yet there are occasions when a life burns more brightly for an instant, and this may attract the attention of one or more gods. The greatest champions and warlords of mortals spend their lives longing for the brief moment that they attract the gaze of the gods, hoping to be granted the power and immortality for which they have strived. Sometimes other events such as cataclysmic wars, the discovery of an ancient artefact or the rise of a new power will also distract a Chaos God from the Great Game. When such a significant occurrence takes place, a Chaos God might pause for a moment to turn a tiny fraction of its attention to events in the physical universe, and will endeavour to influence unfolding events to its own gain. Sometimes a Chaos God will send a Daemon as a messenger, to bring power or information to a mortal. Worshippers of Chaos see such visitations as a blessing from the Dark Powers; god-given quests to be accomplished and righteous wars to be fought. A Chaos God might dispatch a Daemon to retrieve – or place – a certain artefact, or to influence events in such a way that the outcome will bring power to the Chaos God. Across space and time, apparitions and daemonic intrusions have sealed the fates of civilisations, bringing about strife and war, heralding plagues and famine and changing the course of history.

WARP RIFTS
In order for a Daemon to break through into the mortal universe there must be a weakening of the barriers between Warpspace and the material realm – a Warp rift. Some of these occur randomly, other times either the gods or mortals manufacture them. Daemons

constantly seek these weaknesses and fight wars over their possession. The size of the breach can vary tremendously, from a slight thinning of the dimensional walls that allows a Daemon to extend some of its power into the mortal world and possess an individual, to immense tears in reality that massive armies of Daemons use for invasion.

Daemons can possess mortals on the other side of the voidal barrier by transferring some of their power into the mind of their victim. They appear in dreams and visions, and through exploitation of a gap in realities infuse their victim with a portion of their daemonic power. This inevitably leads to the destruction of the possessed mortal, as their physical frame is warped and twisted by the Daemon to suit its own needs and inhuman aesthetic. A few mortals willingly allow themselves to be possessed, glorying in the power and superhuman abilities they gain, even though the energies they crave will eventually destroy them.

Though the physical and psychic power of a Daemon is severely limited by the mortal body it possesses, the scope for mayhem and carnage is still great. Such Daemon-possessed mortals, particularly those who already have power and influence, can start rebellions and wage wars, plunging worlds into centuries of bloodshed and anarchy. The history of the galaxy is littered with devastating conflicts caused by Imperial commanders, army generals and political leaders under a Daemon's influence.

The world of Phalan 10 was subjected to a crippling month-long orbital bombardment under the orders of the Daemon-possessed Admiral Koth. Entire Imperial Guard regiments in transit to warzones have been turned by the power of Chaos when their commanders have been possessed by Daemons. Even some Inquisitors, in studying their enemies too closely, have fallen prey to Daemonic possession, unleashing bloodthirsty witch-hunts and starting costly conflicts, as happened when Inquisitor Vech oversaw the cleansing of the Angelion sector in the late 38th Millennium.

On occasion mortals will perform rituals of summoning. Using hosts or sacrifices, Chaos cultists sometimes create enough of a Warp breach for the essence of a few Daemons to create vessels in the real world. Such manifestations are often weak and short-lived – long enough for the mortals to achieve their purpose, but ultimately transitory and frustrating for the Daemons. While they revel in their physical bodies, the Daemons are servants of the gods and are not happy being bound to the will of mortals or confined within forms that are not their own. Summonings are dangerous to those who perform them, for if a Daemon can break through the wards and protections of the summoners, they can possess or destroy those that sought to cage them.

Often it is the tumultuous movements of the Warp itself that create a break into the material realm, allowing Daemons to spill through the resulting breach. This might happen by chance circumstance; events such as Warp drive implosions and rogue psykers detonating can cause a rift to appear. At other times, the deliberate rituals of mortals can weaken the barriers between realms, allowing the teeming hordes of the Chaos Gods to smash through and enter the material realm. Sometimes, simple suffering, death and misery on a massive scale – as occurs during wars and great calamities – forms a Warpstorm that a daemonic legion can use as a portal.

It does not require much energy for one of the Four to open a breach in the Warp for a single Daemon to enter through the mortal realm. There are times, though, when a whole army of Daemons is required for a momentous quest – a world destroyed, an army smashed asunder, a race wiped out. Rarely will a Chaos God risk the use of so much power, for such extravagance may leave the Chaos God vulnerable. However, at such times when it does unleash such devastating power, whole sectors are swept aside by the tide of Daemons vomited forth upon the unsuspecting galaxy.

Some Warp rifts last mere moments. The Daemonic army becomes immediately trapped in the material realm and will swiftly succumb to the constant leeching of Chaos energy required to maintain its presence in the mortal realm. Warp rifts can also last for days, years and even centuries. Isolated from aid and escape by the perils of the Warpstorm, a world engulfed by a Warp rift becomes the playground and battlefield of the Daemons until the Warp rift finally seals and the Daemons can then be banished back to their everlasting realm. A few Warpstorms have endured so long that they can be considered permanent, their energies self-sustaining.

Of these, the greatest and most dangerous is the Eye of Terror, created by the birth of Slaanesh and home to unnumbered worlds fought over by Daemons and mortals alike, the infamous Traitor Space Marine Legions amongst them. Another significant Warpstorm is the Maelstrom, found near to the galactic core and haven for thousands of pirates and renegades, including the dreaded Red Corsairs. Others, less widely known Warpstorms exist, such as the Heart of Darkness near to the world of Atilla, and the Storm of Judgement that engulfs almost all of the Caradryad sector on the Southern Rim.

DAEMON INVASIONS

A daemonic incursion occurs when an entire army of the Chaos Gods breaks into the material realm. Often strange portents herald this great weakening of the barriers between realms; psykers have waking nightmares, the sky and stars buckle and shift and a feeling of ever-present dread descends upon the hapless world. The rift itself can take many forms. Often it looks like a swirling vortex of kaleidoscopic energy, a seething whirlpool of raw magic. Other times the breach may show a glimpse into the Realm of Chaos beyond, so that maddening vistas of floating towers and screaming trees can be seen, driving mad all those who look upon it. Warp rifts have also appeared as gates of green fire, clouds of impenetrable shadow, boiling lakes of pus and other terrifying visions.

HARLEQUINS

When Slaanesh consumed the Eldar during the Fall, the race became splintered as different factions within their society sought to avoid the hunger of Slaanesh. Perhaps the strangest of all the Eldar who escaped are the Harlequins of the Laughing God.

In the mythology of the Eldar the Laughing God eluded capture when Slaanesh fought with the war god Khaine, and disappeared into the webway. No matter how hard Slaanesh hunts the Laughing God, who is known as Cegorach, the Dark Prince always fails to capture him. The Harlequins are devotees of Cegorach and Eldar legend claims that when they die, the Laughing God steals away their soul before Slaanesh can consume them. The Harlequins do not wear spirit stones to capture their souls upon their deaths, proof enough of their belief that they are protected from the attentions of the Dark Prince.

The Harlequins hate Chaos in all of its forms and often appear to fight against daemonic incursions, guided by their Shadowseers and ancient Eldar prophecies. When they are not fighting, troupes of Harlequins visit the remnants of the Eldar race across the galaxy, and put on entrancing performances of dance and story-telling that warn of the lures of Chaos and tell the dark tale of the Fall of the Eldar.

From out of the roiling Warp rift spill the legions of the Dark Gods. Hordes of Daemons appear, roaring, howling, gibbering and screaming. They fall upon the unfortunate world in a tide of magical destruction. The air around a daemonic host seethes with chaos energy, for the daemonic incursion brings a portion of the Realm of Chaos with it. The ground melts and warps beneath the tread of the Daemons and the sky around them flickers with distant visions. As the Chaos power pours from the rift, matter and energy fuse, turning familiar landmarks into a blistered mass of ever-changing horror.

During an incursion on the hive world of Paraghast, the power of Chaos transformed the principle city of Patrihive into a nightmare. It became a twisted prison to billions of souls, trapping them within a writhing dome of flesh-hungry thorns and creepers twenty kilometres high. Its roots buried into the surrounding ash wastes for a hundred kilometres in every direction, breaking through the ruddy ground to attack the defenders of Paraghast even as they fought against a legion of Nurgle and Slaanesh Daemons.

On the Eldar Exodite world of Menimshemash, the Daemons of Chaos entered through the planet's 'world spirit'. This crystalline psychic network criss-crossed the world, joining together all of the Exodite settlements, housing the souls of their dead from five thousand years of occupation. Tzeentch's realm infiltrated the world spirit and erupted from its deep pathways as monstrous crystal serpents that spewed forth wave after wave of horrific Chaos Daemons.

Daemonic incursions are bizarre and frightening to say the least. Without the physical limitations that restrict mortal armies, a daemonic legion can appear and disappear at will. On occasion, it will mass for a great attack, at other times individual packs of Daemons will hunt across the globe, terrorising the populace, randomly enslaving and killing. Even when the Daemons themselves are elsewhere, a settlement can be plagued by their presence on the same world. Those mortals with even the least psychic potential suffer terribly as the influx of Warp energy unleashes the latent power of their mind; immolating them with magical fire, freezing their blood, turning them into rocky statues, causing arteries to burst or brains to explode. Poltergeist activity and random bursts of devastating telekinesis and pyrokinesis can level buildings and slaughter thousands. People hear cackling voices, deranged screams and lurid whispering, while unnatural stenches and exotic fumes taint the air.

A daemonic invasion is all but impossible to stop by conventional means; the very act of warring against Daemons feeds their power with fear and hatred. Even as the Daemons' forms are destroyed, more of their kind attack through the Warp rift. Only the closing of the Warp rift can deprive the Daemons of their power and allow the daemonic legion to eventually be destroyed.

Often there is nothing that can be done but battle against the incursion to survive the endless days and nights until the Warp rift runs its course.

Once the Warp rift closes, the Daemons are cut off from their unnatural realm and can be hunted down. This is not without its risks, for Daemons that know their time in the world of mortals is ending are spiteful and vicious, eager to cling to their existence for as long as possible. They tend to lash out against anything they encounter, whether warriors or innocents, and are driven into a deadly frenzy of fighting as their doom approaches. It is in these death throes that a daemonic army often causes the most harm, butchering its way across a planet to satisfy its vengeance, heaping untold thousands of souls upon the altars of sacrifice in order to gain as much psychic energy as possible to sustain their weakening presence. During the Voxteth Annihilation, the Daemon known as Skulltaker killed nearly 400 foes in the 48 hours of the daemonic incursion, twice the number of his victims over the previous five months. On Galdemor, the violence committed by the Daemon legion of Braskh'har the Devious, a Herald of Slaanesh, saw thousands slaughtered and caused such grief that a new Warp rift opened, spilling forth the armies of Khal'thar'rak the Bloodied Fang and a host of necrotic Nurgle Daemons

led by Prince Gurglish the Ever-Rotting. The three armies fought over the spoils of the world and left no creature alive by the time they eventually departed back to the Realm of Chaos.

Such battles as are fought against a daemonic incursion are utterly different from those against mortal foes. With the Daemons having complete freedom to move about the engulfed world, rigid battle lines, defensive structures and garrisons have little or no effect. To wage war against invading daemonic hosts, an army must be on its guard at all times, ready to respond to the appearance of its adversaries. To compound matters, Daemons attack for completely different reasons to any mortal race – even the alien Tyranids fight for territory and bio-mass. Instead, the objectives of a Daemon general will often be completely obscure.

Some Daemon armies do have a purpose to achieve, although often it is impossible to guess at the outset. This might be to slay a million mortals, or to retrieve a single artefact. Other times, the Daemons have no goal or plan, and their leaders make decisions according to opportunity and their intrinsic nature.

The Lord of Change Ix'thar'ganix, also known as the Slayer of Destinies, led forth a Daemon legion against the world of Omegath. In his ineffable wisdom, Tzeentch had granted his Greater Daemon a glimpse of a young child born upon the world, who would mature to become a powerful oracle. The Slayer of Destinies craved the power of this child and used all of his magic to open a Warp rift to allow Chaos to spill into Omegath. Yet for all of his prescience, Ix'thar'ganix did not know the location of the child and for twenty days his daemonic hordes swept across Omegath seeking the oracle-to-be.

To the commanders of the defending armies, the Daemons appeared random in their attacks – universities were assaulted, orphanages overwhelmed, palaces destroyed. Unable to comprehend the nature of their foe, the lack of military targets attacked, the soldiers of Omegath fought where they met the Daemons but could not create a plan of their own. The Daemons disappeared mysteriously after twenty days, following an attack on a small farm commune out in the wind-fields. Unknown to the local army chiefs, Ix'thar'ganix had found his prize and stolen the boy's powers of foresight. The populace of Omegath were left bloodied and bemused, ignorant of what had befallen them.

In the 32nd Millennium, the mining colonies of Ichtar IX were cut off from the Imperium for nine hundred years. When the Warpstorm receded nothing remained of the 20,000,000 miners who had lived there. The planet was found devoid of all intelligent life; nothing to testify to the unimaginable agonies the populace must have endured whilst imprisoned by the legions of Chaos. Patrolling fleets and exploratory missions find other such deserted ghost worlds across the Imperium and in wilderness space; bleak reminders of the all-destroying power of Chaos.

DAEMON WORLDS
The power of Chaos infuses worlds trapped within a Warp rift, entwining the impossibilities of the Warp and the realm of the physical. When this corruption is sustained for an age, it creates planets known as Daemon worlds. Daemon worlds straddle the universes, and are as strange as the Realm of Chaos. Like the nightmarish territories of the Dark Powers, Daemon worlds are free from physical constraint, shaped by the emotions of mortals and moulded by the caprice of the world's daemonic rulers.

On the world of Kathalon in the Eye of Terror the Bloodthirster Vangash'hagash the Ever-Bloody holds sway; his world is a great burning lake criss-crossed with arching bridges of brass and bone, over which the legions of Khorne and Tzeentch have fought for aeons.

The World of Immortal Sorrows is a planet ruled over by a Daemon of Slaanesh called Elyssar'sirath. Once at the heart of the ancient Eldar civilisation, it is now a Crone World, where Daemons of the Dark Prince torment the souls of fallen Eldar under the canopy of a great golden forest through which flow rivers made from the tears of Eldar children.

Across the galaxy are many other bizarre and monstrous worlds, where the perverse whims of Daemons hold mortal populations in terrorised thrall and eternal bondage. On other planets, the natives wage endless wars against the legions of Chaos that constantly try to take over their world.

DAEMONS AND THE ELDAR WEBWAY
As the unwitting creators of Slaanesh, the Eldar have a particular loathing for Chaos, and an overwhelming fear of its power. In an age long past, the Eldar learned many secrets of the Warp from the ancient races of the Old Ones. With this knowledge the Eldar created the webway; a pan-galactic network of navigable tunnels that exist within the Warp but also slightly apart from it. At the height of their power, the Eldar could use the webway to travels thousands of light years quickly and safely. It linked all of their worlds, and their starships could move from one end of the galaxy to the other without entering realspace.

When the Fall of the Eldar occurred, much of the webway was destroyed or damaged in the catastrophe. The webway still links the craftworlds upon which the majority of Eldar who escaped the Fall now live, but it is far from safe. The complex psychic wards of its construction fell into disrepair and the Realm of Chaos entered. Chaos energy has overcome vast tracts of the webway and made them impassable.

In other areas, the Eldar still fight back the encroaching Chaos, maintaining their slender links with other craftworlds. On each craftworld there are many portals that are permanently closed with powerful runes of protection; doorways that lead to parts of the webway claimed by Chaos and other perils. Despite these precautions, the webway is still a Daemon's easiest route of entry to a craftworld.

THE WARP UNLEASHED

Chattering and growling filled the great dome of the Ring of Eternal Delights, a deep bowl that seemed hewn from marble yet whose pastel coloured veins constantly shifted from blue to purple to deep red. Here in one of the great wings of the Court of Covenant, a rabble of Daemons all stared up at the apparition hovering in the air above the amphitheatre. Red armoured warriors stalked through the ruins of some strange mortal factory. The Daemons recognised these foes, for they were Space Marines and the stench of the Emperor, the Carrion-Man, hung about them, cloying and filthy.

"Silence!" boomed Anarkh'ad'nron, a huge Bloodthirster who strode through the milling throng, shoving aside Daemons of all shapes and sizes. He cleared a path for a wizened figure, twisted and two-headed, its plumage glistening with magical sparks. Once at the front of the crowd, Fateweaver pulled himself up to his full height.

"Kill them," the Lord of Change said, both heads speaking at once; one spoke in a cackling laugh, the other a sinister whisper. Having made his proclamation, Fateweaver gestured towards the vision of the mortal plane. The edges of the image began to burn with blue fire, growing in strength, opening the gateway to the physical world.

The Daemons jostled forwards in their enthusiasm, a cohort of bestial Bloodletters led by the Herald Deathrender pushing their way to the front. The Space Marines suddenly became aware of the tear in reality and readied their weapons. Deathrender raised his blade above his head and howled a challenge, leading his warriors through the breach into the material universe.

+++ +++ +++

With a lurch they stepped through the portal, drenched by bloody rain, and were immediately engulfed in a storm of small explosions as the Space Marines opened fire with their bolters. Two of Deathrender's cohort shimmered and disappeared in fountains of gore as the detonations tore apart their physical manifestations. Deathrender's blood was up and he cared not for their loss. Behind the foot soldiers of Khorne, Anarkh'ad'nron tore through the portal with a deafening roar, his whip cracking over the backs of the Bloodletters, driving them with feral howls of joy towards the Space Marines.

Laughter drifted past Deathrender as a coterie of Daemonettes leapt nimbly past, skipping across the rubble of the factory without pause.

"Look at the slow fatheads!" tittered their leader, Anatrice, as the lithe Daemons overtook the Bloodletters. "They're going to miss all of the fun!"

A shuffling mass of oozing flesh and pustulent tentacles plopped into existence ahead of Deathrender, blocking his path. He growled whilst Anarkh'ad'nron bellowed at a cringing Herald of Nurgle nearby.

"Get those maggots out of our way!" the Bloodthirster shouted. "Let the red river flow!"

The claws of the Daemonettes were already slicing through the weak joint-guards of the Space Marines and smashing through helmet eye lenses. The Daemonettes giggled infuriatingly as they tossed heads back and forth between them and wrote insults to Khorne in the blood of their victims dripping from the tips of their claws. Deathrender steered his group towards a different target as frag missiles blossomed all around them.

More red-clad Space Marines stood ahead of the Bloodletters, heavy weapons carried upon their shoulders. Deathrender flexed his grip on his Hellblade in anticipation. They were but a dozen strides from their prey when reality tore apart with a thunderous crash. From nowhere, a titanic wall of daemonic flesh and metal crashed into the Space Marines – Bloodcrushers of Hagkhar the Devourer. The huge Juggernauts of Khorne trampled and gored through the Devastators squad, crushing chests and heads while Hagkhar's warriors lopped off limbs and hands. Deathrender put back his head and howled in torment, the urge to kill now so overwhelming that his existence throbbed with deep, insatiable hunger.

Anarkh'ad'nron had found a battle tank to vent his fury upon. His axe chewed a long rent in its hull and sent a sponson spinning into the air, the halved remains of the gunner spattered across the ground. The Bloodthirster's whip wrapped around the tank's main gun, and a pull with godlike thews ripped the turret from the superstructure. Another axe blow and the Predator's fuel tanks exploded. With a triumphant shout, Anarkh'ad'nron bathed in the roaring flames.

Deathrender finally spied a foe no other had yet seen, red-armoured warriors amidst a cluster of soot-slicked chimneys. With a whooping cry, he again raised his blade and signalled the advance, running between flaming craters and the crackling blasts of lascannons.

With a thrust, Deathrender plunged his Hellblade into the chest of a Space Marine with a golden-winged helm. A second stroke separated the head from the body. At the moment of decapitation, exultation surged through Deathrender. The strength of Khorne filled him, as ecstatic destruction flowed around him. Deathrender shook his head, spraying bloody droplets over his warriors, and barked his praises to the Lord of Skulls.

THE DAMNATION OF TOREUS

To be engulfed in a Warp rift is one of the most horrendous fates that can befall a planet. Both the populace and the world itself are twisted and tortured by the Daemons of Chaos. Such was the doom of Toreus.

When contact was re-established with Toreus after it had been cut off by a Warp storm for 300 years, Imperial forces found a world that had been utterly changed. Gone were the thriving metropolises, the verdant farmlands and the towering cathedrals and palaces. In their place stretched warped devastation. Great fissures rent the landscape, filled with bones. Brass towers stretched into the storm-filled skies. Huge mutant beasts hunted through dark forests of petrified trees. The stench of blood and sulphur made men retch. The air itself burnt their eyes and caused their hair to fall out in disgusting clumps.

The cities held horrors of their own. Stretched faces stared from brick and stone, and maze-like alleyways were filled with haunting whispers. The walls were burnt with shadows of men, women and children, which silently writhed in hunch-backed and claw-fingered agony. The sewers heaved with monstrous rats, and fountains of slime and gore burst through the cracked pavements and roadways. Once-golden domes were slicked with filthy verdigris, and crows with blood-matted feathers and glowing red eyes nested under cornices dripping with thick ichor. Statues of Imperial commanders and saints had sprouted horns and wings, and seemed to change position when not looked at.

The chill night brought its own terrors, as the boiling storm clouds parted to reveal a purple moon upon which leered a grinning fanged mouth. Skeletal bats as large as Thunderbolt fighters swooped through the sickly-hued skies. The stars danced and whirled about each other, tracing foul runes with their glittering trails. Bestial howls echoed from the hillsides and the empty streets reverberated to the crunching of teeth gnawing upon bones.

Archeodiviners of the Adeptus Astra Telepathica arrived to investigate what had become of Toreus and the three billion souls who had lived there. As soon as they reached the surface, the psykers were overwhelmed by the residual Chaos tainting the planet. One went mad

THE DESTRUCTION OF TOREUS (COMMENCE 579.M41)

SAKHMET FENS
Once-fertile region, centre of food production. Populace almost eradicated by virulent disease that caused arterial scabbing and intestinal haemorrhages. Pseudospud plantations became festering morass of carnivorous vines that devoured all survivors. Their works will be recorded in the Book of Reprisal.

THEOSAPHUS ORBITAL STATION
Catastrophic implosion. 1.3 million crew lost, presumed dead. We pray for their souls.

AUSEKHLIS
Engulfed for three days by a tornado of blood and body parts. When the city reappeared, buildings and populace had been warped together to create structures of pulsing flesh and splintered bone. 7.8 million dead. Sacrifice is their solace.

DEKLA PENINSULA
Resistance against daemonic incursion concentrated in this area. Refugees and military forces eventually overwhelmed by rampant daemonic host of inestimable size. Approximate casualties: 1.2 billion. Minds with true purpose and faith are never wholly lost.

NILAKANTHA SEA
The island of Kallipus turned into a fanged maw that swallowed and regurgitated the sea once every year.

GORTYZ CITY
The capital of Toreus was assailed by the daemonic horde of the Daemon Prince K'tzis'trix'a'tzar, and eventually mutated into towering columns of crystal and fire. Fate of Imperial Commander Ghorstwenckler unknown. Population of 18.4 million, presumed dead. We offer liturgies for the Emperor to protect their immortal spirits.

MOUNT MAGATHON
Became the fire-scorched dominion of the Daemon Lord An'kha'arak.

TOREUS AT 879.M41
As viewed from the approaching starship *Celestial Conqueror*.

and attacked his fellows; he was only stopped when his head was chopped off. Two others perished miserably, their bodies aging and rotting as if centuries passed with every day. The remaining three were driven insane over the following days as they were assailed by visions of what had befallen the world. To this day Inquisitors pore over the transcripts of the archeodiviners' lunatic ravings and sobbing moans, trying to glean as much knowledge as possible on the foul spawn of the Warp.

CHAOS UNLEASHED
The daemonic attack was heralded by a week of strange portents and omens. In the Temple of the Emperor Sanctified, blood dripped from the claws of the golden eagle above the altar. Astropaths vomited blood and wailed of a great ring of fire burning in the heavens. Birds were seen flying backwards and all the clocks of the city of Geheim stopped at two minutes to midnight. The daughter of Imperial Commander Ghorstwenckler attacked her father and tried to bite out his throat. Rioting mobs filled the streets and the Adeptus Arbites precinct was overrun by a plague of carnivorous toads. At a farm in the hinterlands, a grox was born with the head of a fish and the tail of a lion.

When the Warp rift finally engulfed Toreus it appeared in the skies as a pulsing ring of purple fire. Theosaphus Orbital Station imploded, and high-altitude auguries rained down onto the surface as blazing comets of molten metal. Fires engulfed the Forest of Lassenthus, their flames rising high into the air, and cackling minions of Tzeentch cavorted from the magical inferno. A pool of shadow swallowed the town of Kleist Hollows, as pustulent servants of Nurgle and lascivious Daemons of Slaanesh pulled themselves from its shimmering, oily depths. All across the doomed world portals opened and a host of Daemons poured forth.

A WORLD FALLS
The soldiers of Toreus fought vainly against the rampaging hordes. War raged on the flanks of Toreus' highest volcano, Mount Magathon, as the legion of the Bloodthirster An'kha'arak butchered 50,000 Imperial servants. Great skull-like caves burst from the rocky ground and from their maws rivers of lava poured down onto the beleaguered defenders of Toreus. An army of Bloodletters heaped the skulls of the slain into burning fissures and crimson smog filled the skies. Twisted spires of bone wrought in the shape of dismembered corpses towered from the volcano's summit. Fire and blood engulfed the plains around Mount Magathon, turning farms and towns into gore-drenched cinders. An'kha'arak surveyed his domain, sat upon a brass throne that drifted within the roaring flames at the volcano's peak.

The palaces of the Imperial Commander were besieged by hosts of Pink Horrors, Screamers, Daemonettes and Plaguebearers led by K'tzis'trix'a'tzar, Daemon Prince of Tzeentch. Commander Ghorstwenckler's personal guard retreated with their lord to the inner sanctum of the Palace of Ruminas, but physical defences were no proof against their daemonic foes. Monstrous Juggernauts appeared in the midst of the defenders, trampling and goring with bloody abandon while the Bloodletters riding upon their backs wantonly hacked and slashed at everything within reach. K'tzis'trix'a'tzar stormed through the panicked soldiers at the head of his horde, blasting apart heads and limbs with bolts of blue and pink lightning. The Imperial Commander fell to his knees at the feet of the Daemon Prince and pleaded for his life. K'tzis'trix'a'tzar's cruel laughter echoed around the inner sanctum as the Daemon Prince invoked the name of his master and unleashed a spell of change of unprecedented power.

Mystical flames raged through the citadel, burning everything. From the ashes rose great shards of crystal and jagged mirrors that reflected the warped landscape of the Realm of Chaos. Two twin columns of fire rose into the sky – echoes of the Towers of Helixis that flank the doorway of Tzeentch's library – their flames flickering with the screaming souls of the damned. Between their flaming pinnacles burned a golden sun, which blinded every mortal that looked upon it.

All of Toreus bent and twisted to the insane whims of its daemonic conquerors. Vast mountains of skulls dwarfed the Stratberg Highlands. The city of Chuburis drowned in a lake of blood, and then rose from the depths, its inhabitants choking and covered in gore, only to be drowned again, and again. The cruel laughter of Daemonettes could be heard across the Plains of Antaris as they hunted thousands of humans from the backs of serpentine mounts.

Weeping mortals were caged in bars of smouldering brass and brought out one at a time to be hacked apart by leering Bloodletters. The Tallyman of Nurgle, Epidemius, rounded up millions of refugees and had them incarcerated within a great wall of suppurating flesh. Here he set to cataloguing each and every blemish, spot, boil and pox upon them, before feeding them to a pack of slobbering Beasts of Nurgle.

And then the Warp rift began to falter. Sensing that their grip of this world was beginning to weaken, the Daemons unleashed ever more heinous acts of corruption and depravity. They set to slaughtering every creature they could find, distilling down their essence in immense soul furnaces that blotted out the sun and swathed the world in pitch blackness. The screams of the dying were etched into the rocks themselves, whose shapes were altered by the warping power of Chaos.

Eventually the rift closed and the Daemons vanished, leaving a world changed beyond comprehension. There was nothing left of Toreus as it had been known, and in a rare moment of mercy the planet was virus bombed to remove any vestige of life that might have survived such hideous torment. In the words of Inquisitor Thrax, who was charged with leading the Exterminatus mission:

"Chaos had left its taint in every root, stone and atom. Toreus heaved and wailed in its agonising death throes and we ended its misery. There was nothing else that could be done."

CHAOS AND MANKIND

Without the Warp there would be no psykers, no interstellar travel or communication. The galaxy would be a dark place for Humanity. Yet for all the benefits it brings, the Warp is a place of destruction; the creatures that dwell within prey upon mortals and would see the universe devoured by the Realm of Chaos.

The Warp is essential to the survival of humanity. Spacecraft travel through it, capable of voyaging for thousands of light years. By such means Humanity is bound in a single Imperium, led by the Emperor. Through astrotelepathy and the psychic Navigators, the worlds of the Imperium are able to maintain their fragile bonds. The Emperor's will may be mighty indeed, but his reach is long only because his fleets can travel through Warpspace. While mankind would be a fraction of its current numbers and strength without the Warp, Chaos would also be much diminished without the rise of Mankind. The Chaos Gods drink the emotions and thoughts of Mankind, growing bloated with power in the process. Over the millennia each has fed on an aspect of Man: rage, lust, corruption, and inconstancy. Strengthened and moulded by the thoughts and emotions of reality, the Warp Powers nurture in Mankind those passions that sustain them. As Man has spread across the stars, their numbers have grown immeasurably, fuelling the Chaos Gods. So the circle is established, with Man's follies feeding the Chaos Gods and the Chaos Gods encouraging Man to further follies.

VISIONS OF INSANITY

Few creatures of the material universe can look at the Warp firsthand. Psykers can send their minds into the Warp, for example, while the Navigators of the Imperium have a third eye that allows them to observe the Immaterium from their spacecraft. Even with these supernatural senses, it is impossible to truly see the Warp, for its energy has no substance, no light to refract and reflect, no matter to create scale or distance. Filtered through even the extra senses of a psychic being, the Warp is an analogue created by mortal minds to comprehend the incomprehensible, to instill order and reason on pure chaos. Where there is an infinitely complex interweaving of tidal energies and swirling power, the observer creates a fantastical landscape.

Even these visions have considerable potency and have been known to drive a man to madness, his senses and thoughts utterly inadequate to deal with the phenomenon of the Warp. Castles float through skies of fire, rivers of burning blood pour upwards from smoke-wreathed chasms, and structures of inconceivable geometries push the mind into madness. Behind all of these visions lies the swirling energy of the Warp, constantly feeding on the fear and despair of those who witness its power.

PSYKERS AND THE WARP

Warpspace has many strange properties, most of which remain a mystery to the research cosmologians of the Adeptus Mechanicus and Adeptus Astra Telepathica. Humanity has long been able to use the power of the Warp – magicians, seers, witches, mediums, shamans and exorcists have all tapped into its power, although most likely they have done so without a true understanding of their abilities. In the 41st Millennium these individuals are known as psykers. Psykers use their powers by drawing upon the Warp, using their minds to siphon its unnatural energy to hurl blasts of power, teleport objects, send their thoughts across space and perform countless other 'miracles'.

Once, the 'gift' of psychic power was rare, confined to only a few helpless individuals who usually fell victim to superstitious prejudice. However the number of psykers has risen with every passing century, now as high as one in every few thousand souls on some planets. This massive increase in psychic activity constitutes a profound danger to humanity. Every time a psyker draws upon the Warp, he disturbs its flow, creating an eddy that may simply die away or be fed by other movements until it becomes a raging tempest that feeds a Chaos God. Each psyker causes a pinprick of disturbance within the Warp; each can be the seed of a Warpstorm; each can rouse a Chaos Power.

THE TEMPTATIONS OF CHAOS

In an Imperium that is harsh and unforgiving, power is held by a few and the majority of citizens live in a numbing existence of drudgery and depredation. Yet no matter how broken a man's will is, how much the lash scars his back, there remains a spark of hope, of a desire for something more. Power is all but impossible to gain by conventional means, yet there are other ways to rise to prominence…

Chaos Daemons are well aware of these weaknesses and fully exploit them in order to extend their control over the universe on behalf of their masters. Tempting mortals with the reward of power in return for worship, they recruit millions of devoted and fanatical followers – uncountable hordes on innumerable worlds, throughout the vast gulfs of space and time, ready to obey the Chaos Gods' every whim and command. Even in death, the souls of these mortals who have dedicated their lives to a Chaos God are claimed by their patron power.

Even the great feats of the most successful Chaos Champions only attract the attention of their patron for a brief instant, maybe enough for the god to grant

ORDO MALLEUS THE GREY KNIGHTS

Such is the threat of daemonic intrusion that there is a whole branch of the Emperor's Inquisition dedicated to seeking out and destroying Daemons. This is the Ordo Malleus, known as the Daemon Hunters.

Most Daemon hunters are learned in many aspects of Daemon Lore, in particular the signs of daemonic possession, rituals and symbols, and the spoor of daemonic activity. They are also highly trained in the ways in which Daemons can be banished back to the Warp, and to this end are armed with many bizarre weapons and items of wargear created solely for this purpose.

The Ordo Malleus has a Chamber Militant comprising an entire Chapter of Space Marines. These are the Grey Knights, the cutting edge of the Emperor's Daemon-killing sword. All Grey Knights are psykers who have been tested and found strong enough to resist the power and temptations of Daemons. Led by the Justicars, Grey Knights are deployed to fight Daemons all across the galaxy, purging their presence with Nemesis force weapons and blessed flamers.

the loyal follower a gift of mutation or a mighty weapon to further its works. Ever so rarely, however, the Gods might bestow that one prize every Champion covets – to be lifted from his mortal condition into the Realm of Chaos, to be reborn in mind and body as a mighty Daemon Prince.

DOOM AND DAMNATION
Only a learned few amongst Mankind know the true threat of Chaos, and have learned from the doom of others just what can happen to a race that succumbs to the lure of Chaos. Shattered worlds and long-forgotten civilisations dot the galaxy as testament to whole species that fell into damnation or destroyed themselves in the service of Chaos. Of these, the greatest were the Eldar – a race that once spanned the galaxy, now reduced to a few survivors adrift upon the cold void.

There are some Eldar, those not too prepossessed with their own woes and struggles for survival, who see in Mankind the same peril that destroyed their race. For these individuals, Mankind is a reminder of what happened long ago. Humanity is treading the same path towards the darkness of Chaos, a crude mirror of the Eldar's own disgrace. All the signs are there for those with the wit and experience to see them. The growth of mutation, the ever-increasing numbers of psykers and the swelling legions of those sworn to the Dark Gods all point towards the impending cataclysm. Should the weaknesses of Mankind prove too great, one only needs to look at the Fall of the Eldar to see the consequences of failure.

The teeming thousands of trillions of humans spread across the galaxy provide an unmatched source of psychic energy to feed the Chaos Gods. As Humanity

evolves towards its psychic potential, the threat of Chaos grows greater with every passing generation. There is but one reason why Mankind has not already been plunged into a nightmare age of slavery to the Dark Gods of Chaos – the Emperor. Only through the strength and sacrifice of the Emperor are the most dangerous predations of Chaos kept at bay.

THE EMPEROR
The Immortal Emperor of Mankind is the shield and saviour of Humanity. He has sat, held immobile within the Golden Throne, for 10,000 years. Through his powerful mind and the unconquerable might of his will, the Emperor shields humanity from the worst depredations of Chaos. His mind directs the Astronomican-beacon for spacecraft; his will binds the Imperium together and guides his followers through the Emperor's Tarot; he is a god and father to his race. He has sacrificed himself, giving up his endless life to the service of Man. The price to pay is high, for the Emperor must feed constantly upon the souls of his loyal subjects – millions of psykers every year are sacrificed to the artifices of the Golden Throne that sustain His immortal presence.

It is impossible to say for how long the Emperor can survive in this condition, or even if he has survived at all. Who can know how much time is left to him before the tenuous hold upon his physical body is finally broken, or his mind is torn apart by insanity? Such a fate is best not contemplated, for without the Emperor's protection, Mankind would be scattered and alone in the darkness, utterly helpless before the dark temptations of Chaos. Humanity's damnation would bring about the victory of the Dark Gods and the Realm of Chaos would engulf the galaxy.

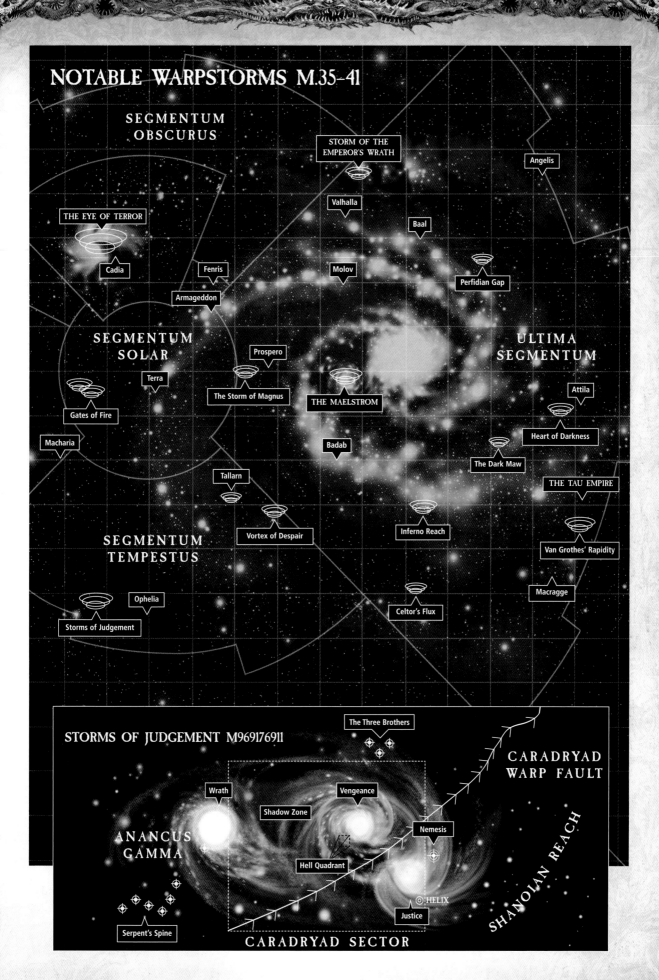

NOTABLE WARPSTORMS M.35–41

SEGMENTUM OBSCURUS

STORM OF THE EMPEROR'S WRATH

Angelis

Valhalla

Baal

THE EYE OF TERROR

Cadia

Fenris

Molov

Perfidian Gap

Armageddon

SEGMENTUM SOLAR

ULTIMA SEGMENTUM

Prospero

Terra

The Storm of Magnus

THE MAELSTROM

Attila

Gates of Fire

Heart of Darkness

Macharia

Badab

The Dark Maw

THE TAU EMPIRE

Tallarn

SEGMENTUM TEMPESTUS

Vortex of Despair

Inferno Reach

Van Grothes' Rapidity

Macragge

Ophelia

Storms of Judgement

Celtor's Flux

STORMS OF JUDGEMENT M969176911

The Three Brothers

CARADRYAD WARP FAULT

Wrath

Vengeance

Shadow Zone

Nemesis

ANANCUS GAMMA

Hell Quadrant

SHANOLAN REACH

⊙ HELIX

Justice

Serpent's Spine

CARADRYAD SECTOR

THE FALL OF KHER-YS

There came a time when Slaanesh's eye fell upon a gleaming gem that he desired. Kher-Ys this jewel was named; an Eldar craftworld rich in souls and drifting dangerously close to the Eye of Terror. As Slaanesh coveted this thing, so too did his minions, and a great many gathered to seize their share of the prize.

Yet Kher-Ys was protected. Wards of energy sealed the craftworld from the Webway, and warriors patrolled the Silver River that led to her gates. Unable to take what they desired, the Daemons of Slaanesh assembled around Kher-Ys, and spoke with enchanting voices to those within. Many ignored the siren calls, but a few were lured from the sanctuary of their craftworld, their spirits fired with whispers of decadent adventure.

One in particular attracted the gaze of Ail'Slath'Sleresh, a Keeper of Secrets, known also as the Heartslayer. The Eldar girl's innocent soul blazed in the Warp, but at its heart there was a dark shadow. Its flickering enigma entranced Heartslayer and the Daemon resolved that in this Eldar's spirit lay the key to taking Kher-Ys. The Greater Daemon travelled onto the Silver River clad in the guise of an Eldar male, and bewitched the maiden with every glamour and guile in his possession. She loved her new companion as only an Eldar can love, and in time Heartslayer persuaded her to return with him to her home.

With his unnatural presence swathed in the love of the Eldar, Heartslayer was able to pass through the barriers of Kher-Ys, and he stole within, seeking the opportunity to strike. The great portal that led to the Silver River was held fast by a psychic key, which lay in the possession of the maiden's father, an Autarch of Kher-Ys. While the Eldar slumbered, Heartslayer stole the key from about his neck and opened the wards upon the Webway.

As a vicious flock, the Daemons of Slaanesh descended upon Kher-Ys. Daemonettes fell upon the Aspect Shrines with illusion and claw, and cast over the altars of twisted Khaine. The Masque weaved her deadly dance with the Howling Banshees, ever eluding their glowing blades as she cut and slashed with her dextrous claws. Huntresses mounted on their serpentine steeds ran rampant through the arcing forest domes, tearing apart green-clad Guardians. Though shurikens and Warp energy tore the air, the chilling cries of the Daemonettes did not diminish, but instead grew in strength as more and more of their kind rushed through the broken gateway.

Heartslayer showed his true form, a mighty creature that towered above the Eldar, and they fled from his terrifying visage. The Keeper of Secrets was drawn to the heart of Kher-Ys, where still slumbered the Avatar of Khaine, the incarnation of Kher-Ys' warrior spirit.

Heartslayer gloated over its dormant form, and ran his claws over the cold iron of its body. Inert and helpless, the Avatar sat motionless and unmoved by the Greater Daemon's caresses. Then some spark awoke in the Avatar's spirit, roused by the death and destruction wrought upon Kher-Ys. Fuelled by the instinct to kill and destroy, the Avatar blazed into life, and seized Heartslayer in its unbreakable grip. With a laugh, the Greater Daemon sheared off the bloodied fist about his throat, and blinded the Avatar with swift strikes to its burning eyes. Its heat crackled over the Keeper of Secret's immortal flesh and washed through his spirit, invigorating his desire to possess this thing. Awakened but untamed, the Avatar was a soulless thing, and Heartslayer saw opportunity in its hollowness. The Greater Daemon invested himself into the shell of the Avatar, and perverted it from within. Bursting forth with borrowed form, the Keeper of Secrets blazed with the sacred fire. Led by their burning demigod, the Daemons of Slaanesh gorged themselves on the Eldar of Kher-Ys for many days and nights. Thousands fell to their insatiable thirsts, and Slaanesh claimed his prized jewel.

So now Kher-Ys drifts the outer eddies of the Eye of Terror empty and desolate, its corridors still ringing with the death cries of its people and the laughter of their slayers.

DAEMONIC FORCES

On the following pages are the complete rules for the models in the Chaos Daemons army. Each entry includes the model's characteristics profile, its special rules, and any unique wargear it is equipped with. This first page lists the more generic army rules.

DAEMON

This special rule applies to every model in this army and includes the following four special rules:

Fearless

The incomprehensible minds of the denizens of the Warp are not subject to the terrors that plague mortals.

Every model in the army is Fearless, as described in the Warhammer 40,000 rule book.

Invulnerable!

The mightiest weapons in the arsenal of mortal armies are often powerless against the supernatural defences of the fiends from the Immaterium.

Every model in the army has the Eternal Warrior universal special rule (see the Warhammer 40,000 rule book) and is therefore immune to Instant Death.

In addition, if the profile of a model in this army includes a Save (Sv) characteristic, this is its Invulnerable save. Some models may also have an armour save, but this will be noted separately in their entry.

Daemonic Assault

Daemons do not go to war in the same way as mortals, rather, guided by the capricious will of their Dark Gods, they appear out of thin air, reality screaming as it is torn apart by the baleful energies of the Warp.

No model in this army is ever placed on the battlefield during deployment. Instead, all of the units in the army always start the game in reserve, even in missions that do not normally allow this rule to be used. You must declare if any independent characters are on their own, counting as a separate unit in reserve, or if they are joining a unit, in which case they and their unit are a single unit in reserve. The enemy deploys as normal.

At the beginning of your first turn, divide the army into two groups that must include, as much as possible, the same number of units. Then you must face the unfathomable judgement of the Gods of Chaos, and nominate which of the two groups you wish to make a 'Daemonic Assault' at the beginning of the battle. Pick one of the two groups and pray to the Dark Gods by rolling a D6. On a 3-6 the Powers of Chaos agree with your choice, but on a 1-2 they choose the other group.

The units in the group that has been chosen to make the Daemonic Assault arrive on your first turn, using the Deep Strike rules. The remaining units are held in reserve and their arrival is rolled for as normal. When a unit becomes available, it enters play by Deep Strike.

Daemonic Rivalry

So bitter is the enmity amongst the Dark Powers that it is unthinkable for their Heralds to lead rival Daemons.

Independent characters in this list cannot join units of Daemons belonging to a different Chaos God or units of Furies of Chaos.

DAEMONIC GIFTS

The most important of Daemons are granted exceptional powers by their Patron God.

Daemons do not have wargear like mortals do, but instead have Daemonic Gifts. Some Daemons can be given additional Daemonic Gifts at the cost given in their entry in the Army List which can be found on pages 77-87. A complete list of Daemonic Gifts and their rules can be found on page 73-76.

BLOODTHIRSTERS
THE RAGE OF KHORNE INCARNATE

Nothing, on any of the many battlefields of the war-ridden 41st Millennium, can match the fury and fighting prowess of the Greater Daemons of Khorne, the dreaded Bloodthirsters. No one, not even the Greater Daemons of the other Dark Gods, can hope to defeat a Bloodthirster at close quarters. Nowhere, in an entire galaxy of worlds at war can a deadlier opponent be found by glory seeking fools.

Bloodthirsters are the perfect embodiment of Khorne's infinite anger, of his unparalleled martial discipline and of his inextinguishable lust for blood. They are the commanders of Khorne's legions, leading them into battle and unleashing the blood-hungry hordes of their master without mercy or compassion, and yet with an implacable tactical efficiency.

Bloodthirsters appear as muscular giants, towering above mortal and Daemon alike, with snarling, bestial faces with long fangs, a wild mane and wickedly sharp horns. They have great leathery wings that carry them majestically across the battlefield in search of more enemies to slaughter, in the vain hope of meeting an opponent worthy of their prowess.

They wear ancient, ornamented armour of brass and wrought iron, upon which the glowing-red runes of Khorne attest the favour of the Blood God. These are a solid bulwark against both treacherous psychic powers and cowardly ranged weapons that their puny enemies often employ in a desperate attempt at bringing them down at a distance. And indeed this tactic is often an opponent's only chance, because if a Bloodthirster manages to close in and engage his enemies in mêle, their fate is sealed.

As well as the razor-sharp claws on their mighty hands, the Greater Daemons of Khorne carry great axes, forged in the heat of the rage of the Lord of War and imbued with the essence of caged Greater Daemons. Perhaps the most fearful weapons ever created, these gigantic axes can cleave battle tanks in two or hamstring a charging Carnifex with a single blow. Not only they destroy a foe's body, but often consume his soul too, offering them to the Lord of Battle.

Obsessed with dealing as much death and destruction as possible in the name of their demanding god, the Bloodthirsters hunger to deal death to their foes, even at range. To this end they can strike down a distant foe with a long barbed whip, throwing axes or simply the shattering power of their deafening bellow. These weapons, though not as satisfying as cleaving apart a foe with a hefty axe-blow, do allow the Bloodthirster to reach and destroy even the fastest and most agile opponents – those that might be wisely trying to keep their distance.

	WS	BS	S	T	W	I	A	Ld	Sv
Bloodthirster	10	4	7	6	4	5	5	10	4+

Unit Type:
Monstrous Creature.

Daemonic Gifts:
Iron Hide, Daemonic Flight.

Special Rules:
Daemon, Furious Charge.

"Gut them! Slaughter them!
Slay them! Butcher them!
Kill! Kill! Kill!
Never stop, never tire!
Keep doing the Lord's work!"

Khar-Har the Undefeatable

KEEPERS OF SECRETS
BRINGERS OF SLAANESH'S TEMPTATIONS

There is nothing so loathsome yet beguiling as a Keeper of Secrets. Wreathed in glamours and mind-dulling musks, this monstrous beast masks its true form with supernatural allure. More than any other Greater Daemon, the appearance of a Keeper of Secrets can vary wildly from its fellows. Created by the capricious whim of Slaanesh, each is a unique statement of the Dark Prince's particular mood and muse at the time of its creation. Some Keepers of Secrets have haunting, androgynous faces pierced with rings, with fanged mouths from which forked tongues flicker. Diaphanous robes swirl around their bodies, floating in a scented witch-breeze that befuddles the senses. Others are more bestial, wide-eyed and fierce, decked in fine scale armour or plates of black-lacquered hide pierced with glittering studs and gems. All of them, however, are several times the height of a man, with jewel-like eyes and sinuous movements, and they all have a splendid crown of horns.

All sensation is a blessing to a Keeper of Secrets, for the thrill of fear is as exquisite as the triumph of victory. To a Keeper of Secrets, pain is simply another sensation to be bestowed on others, or to be enjoyed when others inflict it. The great servants of the Lord of Pleasure feed upon the rampaging hope and dread of their enemies, suckling life from terror and leeching energy from despair. They are despoilers of purity, liking nothing more than to take the noble ideals of others and twist them to selfish ambition and self-satisfaction. The Keepers of Secrets exist to dash dreams and fulfil nightmares, growing strong on the impulsive emotions of those that fight them.

The Greater Daemons of Slaanesh consider battle as another form of creative expression, taking delight in the interplay of explosions, blood and horror, feeding upon the strong emotions triggered by mortals that are torn apart. The pleas for mercy of the wounded and the battle cries of the fighters are music to the Daemon's ears, a delectable opera in honour of its Master. Lithe and deadly, a Keeper of Secrets has long claws that it uses to eviscerate opponents, spilling their blood in pleasing patterns, spreading limbs and organs in exotic, interweaving tapestries of death.

As well as being a vicious warrior, a Keeper of Secrets possesses knowledge of many mystical arts. Weaving spells of misdirection and mystification, it leads the weak to their doom and sends the strong on fools' errands. It invades the thoughts and senses of its enemies, it penetrates their every defence, sending them visions of glory, titillating their egos, caressing their inner desires to lead them astray. There is nothing more satisfying for a Keeper of Secrets than to corrupt a warrior of pure heart and noble intent, turning his quest for glory into a sacrifice upon the altar of Slaanesh's perverse will.

	WS	BS	S	T	W	I	A	Ld	Sv
Keeper of Secrets	8	4	6	6	4	10	6	10	4+

Unit Type:
Monstrous Creature.

Daemonic Gifts:
Aura of Acquiescence.

Special Rules:
Daemon, Fleet.

"Pools of blood glisten so brightly.
Death cries echo so harmoniously.
We drink deeply of fear and pain.
Only thus we can soothe our fiery hearts."

Illaitanen, Handmaiden of Slaanesh

GREAT UNCLEAN ONES
NURGLE'S LORDS OF BOUNTEOUS FILTH

The immense, bloated Greater Daemons of Nurgle tower above the babbling hordes of Nurgle like corpulent schoolmasters. Alternately jovial and stern, a Great Unclean One commands his legion with affectionate bellows of praise and bombastic cajoling. Fuelled by morbid energy, a Great Unclean One pays careful attention to all of his followers, delighting in the smallest boil, revelling in the variety and effulgence of their poxes. With gurgling guffaws, the Greater Daemon sends forth his legions with extravagant waves of his arms, extolling the virtues of plague and pestilence, booming words of encouragement or reproach across the battlefield.

It is not just the forthright personality of a Great Unclean One that gives him so much presence. Each is a huge creature shaped in the fashion of Nurgle; massively rotund, his fleshy form torn with rotting splits, his innards spilling into view as he strides forward. Clusters of buboes erupt from his green hide, birthing small swarms of Nurglings. Noxious juices seep from dozens of sores, leaving a glistening trail of mucus and filth in the Great Unclean One's wake. Fractured, lichen-mottled antlers sprout from the Great Unclean One's head, often hung with festive garlands of

decaying intestines. Globules of yellowy-green spittle fly from his wide mouth as the Great Unclean One urges his minions onwards. Pallid maggots feed upon the Great Unclean One's exposed flesh, growing into furry, thick-bodied flies that form a dark swarm around the Greater Daemon. Filled with unholy vitality, a Great Unclean One is impervious to pain and physical wounds have little effect on it; plasma-burnt flesh quickly transforms into suppurating scars, bullet wounds become oozing pockmarks and tissue shredded by las-blasts forms into warty, crusted scabs.

As monstrous and horrific as his appearance is, a Great Unclean One is possessed of a paternal affection at odds with his nightmarish form. Gregarious and sentimental, a Great Unclean One takes pride in the achievements of his followers, and looks upon all the creatures in his legion as his 'children'. Driven to organise Nurgle's chaotic endeavours, the Great Unclean Ones seek to instil purpose and function on the daemonic rabble they command. With vociferous proclamations, a Great Unclean One heaps praise upon those who spread disease and filth, who butcher the enemy and infect their corpses. With chiding grumbles, the Greater Daemon harries those who are tardy in advancing or who seem less energetic in the pursuit of Nurgle's goals.

Just as spreading disease and decay fills a Great Unclean One with jovial vigour, opposing Nurgle's great schemes rouses tremendous, righteous ire. Though ponderous, a Great Unclean One is all but unstoppable on the advance, wading into the enemy through even the fiercest firepower. Whether armed with a rusted plagueblade encrusted with the festering blood of thousands, or swinging a flail made of skulls filled with burning ichor, a Great Unclean One flattens its foes with its fury. The Great Unclean One unleashes its 'stream of corruption' against those that try to flee its wrath, vomiting forth a steaming tide of virulent filth, maggots and mucus that sweeps away the enemies of Chaos.

	WS	BS	S	T	W	I	A	Ld	Sv
Great Unclean One	6	4	6	6	5	2	4	10	4+

Unit Type:
Monstrous Creature.

Daemonic Gifts:
Noxious Touch.

Special Rules:
Daemon, Slow & Purposeful, Feel No Pain.

LORDS OF CHANGE
TZEENTCH'S SUPREME MUTATORS

The Lords of Change, Greater Daemons of Tzeentch, often appear as tall and slender humanoids, with a long neck and a bird-like head. They are attired in a high wizard's robe and ornaments, and carry a sorcerer's staff in their taloned hands. They have mighty wings with multi-coloured feathers, which allow them to soar high in the sky to carry out their god's orders. Tzeentch's areas of influence are magic, deception and knowledge. His Greater Daemons are the personification of all of these.

Magic. Lords of Change are the most powerful sorcerers in the galaxy, gifted with unparalleled psychic abilities and a near-infinite skill and expertise in the arcane sciences. They can turn scores of mortals to boneless spawn with a mere glance, destroy an armoured vehicle with the flick of a finger or wrench the soul out of the mouth of the mightiest of warriors with a simple word, only to devour it with the delight of a connoisseur. Magic is the power to change – to change matter into energy, unliving into living, lead into gold, and the opposite of all these. Magic is change and change is magic, and both are boons from their Master, the Changer of the Ways.

Deception. To cheat, scheme and manoeuvre in order to gain an advantage over one's enemies, or peers, is one of the most practiced activities in the entire galaxy. From the corridors of the Administratum on Terra, to the high spires of the Eldar Craftworlds, from the bridges of battle barges in the Eye of Terror, to the palaces of planetary governors, mortals are always busy plotting against one another, striking deals with so-called allies only to then stab them in the back when their usefulness has come to an end. Lords of Change revel in these activities. They fuel them, nurture them, concoct them with all of their unmatched guile. They often assume the guise of mortals only to lead these ambitious, influential individuals to lose their soul, often together with the rest of their home world.

Knowledge. The mind of a Lord of Change is an inexhaustible well of information, so much so that to mortals these Daemons appear omniscient. The most unnerving of their abilities, however, is their prescience. Their Great Master, who knows all, has granted them the boon of seeing into the near future, a power that makes them almost impossible to defeat. How can one fight against an enemy that knows in advance every move and every trick you are going to attempt? A Lord of Change can be brought down by the weapons of mere mortals, but only when its demise is part of Tzeentch's schemes, and the Ultimate Deceiver tricks his own Daemon by sending it false visions of the future. Because of this, the destruction of a Lord of Change should bring no joy to the enemy, as they are only helping the Changer of the Ways to move his pawns on the board of the Great Game.

	WS	BS	S	T	W	I	A	Ld	Sv
Lord of Change	5	5	6	6	4	5	3	10	3+

Unit Type:
Monstrous Creature.

Daemonic Gifts:
Daemonic Flight, Soul Devourer, Bolt of Tzeentch, Daemonic Gaze.

Special Rules:
Daemon.

> "Curiosity begets knowledge.
> Knowledge begets curiosity.
> Only great Tzeentch sates both."
>
> *The Teachings of Tz'Kul'Anak*

BLOODLETTERS
THE WARMONGERS OF KHORNE

The Bloodletters are the Lesser Daemons of Khorne and form the core of the vast Legions of the Lord of Battle. They are his unstoppable warriors and amongst the deadliest fighters in the galaxy. Their skin is the colour of red-gore, pleasing to their patron; their bodies are humanoid in shape with bestial snarling faces, burning pupil-less eyes and horned elongated craniums, reminiscent of great war-helms. The strength of their long sinewy limbs is infamous, as is the ferocity of their charges and the grim battle lust with which they tear apart anybody who stands before them. An overwhelming stench of blood always accompanies them like a dark pall, as they march to battle to the sound of drums and war-horns.

Bloodletters are armed with dreaded Hellblades, great two-handed weapons as sharp as Khorne's hatred. Legend has it that each Hellblade has the soul of an angry Daemon trapped inside it. Be that as it may, it is a fact that no armour forged by mortals can withstand the assault of these dark swords, and the sight of their own comrades cut in half by a single stroke of a howling Bloodletter is enough to break the nerve of the stoutest soldiers.

Unlike other Daemons, Bloodletters march to war in regimented formations, for their creator is the Lord of Battle and they are united in the cause of spilling blood. Lines of Bloodletters manoeuvre in several ranks with supernatural precision, or congregate in disciplined maniples advancing in echelon. These formations quickly break up after contact with the enemy however, as individual Bloodletters compete with each other in the taking of enemy heads and spilling the enemy's vital fluids. Each Daemon tries as hard as possible to gain the favour of the Blood God by distinguishing itself in the eyes of their leaders – the dreaded Heralds of Khorne.

The Heralds are the largest and most senior of the Bloodletters. They are rampaging combat masters, capable of single-handedly taking down entire squads of lowlier fighters in a show of martial skill and sheer violence that only the best mortal warriors can hope to match. Some of these Daemon-officers are powerful enough that they can thrust their wailing Hellblade into the armoured hull of enemy battle tanks, tearing apart steel plates and armoured hatches in their frenzied eagerness to reach the inside of the machines and butcher their crew.

	WS	BS	S	T	W	I	A	Ld	Sv
Bloodletter	5	0	4	4	1	4	2	10	5+
Herald of Khorne	6	3	4	4	2	5	3	10	5+

Unit Type:
Infantry.

Daemonic Gifts:
Hellblades.

Special Rules:
Daemon, Furious Charge.
Heralds are also Independent Characters.

"Slay without pity; triumph without remorse.

You are the legions of Khorne, His favourite warriors.

You shall bring defeat and death to His enemies.

You shall crush their worlds under your heel.

To battle! Let blood flow in His name!"

Rorath'rath the Skullwearer

DAEMONETTES
MAIDENS OF SLAANESH'S ECSTASY

Most numerous of Slaanesh's servants are his Lesser Daemons, the Daemonettes. They serve as courtiers and courtesans in the Palace of Pleasure, created to fulfil Slaanesh's every passing whim. They fill Slaanesh's throne room, lounging upon long divans and silken cushions, gossiping endlessly, scheming to earn greater favour from their master.

In appearance the Daemonettes are both beautiful and repulsive. They have slender, clean-limbed bodies with pale, smooth skin, and an androgynous charm that is heightened by the scent of the musk that glistens from their sleek bodies. Instead of hands, the Daemonettes have long, dextrous claws, with which they can bestow the gentlest caress or a deadly slash with equal skill. They have bird-like feet, and move swiftly with languid strides of their long legs. Their faces are genderless masks, dominated by opal eyes that bewitch any who look into them. Their true appearance matters little, however, because they are surrounded by the bewitching aura of their Master. This supernatural power makes them always appear as the ultimate beauty and object of desire in the eyes of their unfortunate enemies, regardless of their race, gender or morality.

The Daemonettes are Slaanesh's warriors and messengers beyond his realm. Slaanesh is given to swift changes of mood, and when frustrated he lashes out with his legions, sending his Daemonettes to obliterate everything he finds repugnant, unsubtle and crude, and replacing them with artistic vistas of destruction. The Daemonettes are vicious, merciless fighters who attack with astounding speed and grace, tearing apart their foes with sweeping, artistic strokes of their razor-sharp claws.

Sometimes Slaanesh is more delicate in his machinations, seeking to undermine the will of his foes, tempting them from their chosen path and removing their opposition to his cause. Slaanesh will also despatch a Daemonette to corrupt his enemies. Using her seductive spells, the Daemonette whispers into the dreams and nightmares of her victim, fuelling their darkest desires. With promises of glory and self-fulfilment, the Daemonette twists the aspirations and ambitions of their prey into self-obsession, paranoia and madness, luring the victim onto the indulgent road towards self-destruction.

The more privileged a Dameonette is – the more she pleases the Dark Prince – the closer to his throne she is allowed to approach. The most favoured Daemonettes are the handmaidens, fastest and most deadly of his courtesans. Also known as the Heralds of Slaanesh, these handmaidens are allowed on to Slaanesh's dais to feed him delicacies and stroke his body with their oiled claws.

	WS	BS	S	T	W	I	A	Ld	Sv
Daemonette	4	0	3	3	1	6	3	10	5+
Herald of Slaanesh	5	3	3	3	2	7	4	10	5+

Unit Type:
Infantry

Daemonic Gifts:
Aura of Acquiescence, Rending Claws.

Special Rules:
Daemon, Fleet. Heralds are also Independent Characters.

> "Hope, love, hate. All are but desire by other names. Thus it is that desire is always foremost amongst the concerns of mortals, and through their desires we shall lead them into our benighted paradise."
>
> *Proclamations of Elsand'daa'arai*

PLAGUEBEARERS
ROTTEN PALADINS OF NURGLE

depraved scientists who create ever-more debilitating illnesses to inflict upon their enemies. Within rotting mounds of corpses Nurgle's eternal energy creates new fungal spores and births new breeds of necrotic bacilli.

The Plaguebearers are solemn, efficient fighters whose Plagueswords can fell the mightiest enemies with a single infected cut. Unfeeling of pain, Plaguebearers fight with a grim vigour that traps their foes in a gruelling war of attrition – a war that only the servants of the Lord of Decay can win.

Plaguebearers are formed from the energy of mortals that died from Nurgle's Rot, the Lord of Decay's most virulent and deadly blessing. The souls of those infected by this disease are slowly leeched into Nurgle's realm, appearing as warty seed pods growing from the cracked branches of gloomy willows. Each pod swells and ripens as the Nurgle's Rot destroys its host in the real world and the nascent Plaguebearer feeds upon the victim's dying energies.

These pods emit a sickly aroma whilst turning into a pustule of excreta within which writhes the growing Plaguebearer. When fully matured, the podule drops into the mulch and the newly created Plaguebearer tears himself from the leathery cocoon. A mortal who resists the ravages of the Nurgle's Rot for a significant period creates an equally long incubation period for their resultant Daemon, and this will grow into a Herald of Nurgle; a larger, tougher and more disgusting individual amongst the deformed masses of the Plaguebearers.

Sonorous chanting and the dull knell of bells herald the arrival of Nurgle's Plaguebearers. Surrounded by a buzzing swarm of flies, the Plaguebearers shuffle forwards, their bodies broken and twisted with morbidity. Bloated stomachs tear through paper-thin skin, showing glistening guts dripping with foetid liquids. Rheumy, cyclopean eyes stare from haggard, ravaged faces topped by a single broken horn blackened with filth. Gangling, bony limbs propel the Plaguebearers forward in a staggering lope, fuelled by the energy of decay. In their hands the Plaguebearers grasp rusted blades; Plagueswords dripping with noxious infection.

The constant humming of flies is mixed with the monotonal chants of the Lesser Daemons of Nurgle; each attempting to count the number of plagues, diseases and poxes gifted to the universe by great Nurgle. These are the Tallymen of Nurgle, eternally bound to record all of the Plague God's pestilential gifts. It is an impossible task, for Nurgle's bountiful enthusiasm knows no bounds and every day sees new strains of viruses and freshly evolved bacteria spreading across the realm of mortals. In hidden laboratories, the whispers of Nurgle's wisdom fills the minds of

	WS	BS	S	T	W	I	A	Ld	Sv
Plaguebearer	3	0	4	5	1	2	1	10	5+
Herald of Nurgle	4	3	4	5	2	3	2	10	5+

Unit Type:
Infantry.

Daemonic Gifts:
Plaguesword.

Special Rules:
Daemon, Slow & Purposeful, Feel No Pain.
Heralds are also Independent Characters.

> "All things must wither and die. Let root rot and bower blight, to feed the pestilence of abandoned hope."
>
> *Aghalhor the Bringer of Poxes*

PINK HORRORS
CORUSCATING SPELLBINDERS OF TZEENTCH

Pink Horrors are possibly the most bizarre of all Daemons. They have stubby, pink bodies with long, gangly arms and legs, and no head. Their leering faces appear normally in the middle of their chest, but can vanish at any moment, only to reappear on their back, in their joined hands or some other equally unpredictable part of their anatomy.

They group together in cheerful, colourful mobs, which dance and cavort erratically across the battlefield to the rhythm of their own cacophonous humming. As they advance, cackling madly at their own incomprehensible jokes, they casually unleash a barrage of arcane missiles of ever-changing hues, mutating the best-protected enemies into blobs of gelatinous flesh.

Even though they are completely useless at any form of hand-to-hand combat, Pink Horrors are difficult opponents to get rid of. Even more than other Daemons, they seem immune to the effects of the most powerful enemy weapons, regenerating missing limbs with nonchalant ease. When finally a skilled enemy manages to hit them full-square in the chest or to cut them in half with a well-placed blow, Pink Horrors reveal their most unique form of defence.

The Daemon simply splits into two halves, which reshape themselves into two smaller copies of the original. These two new Daemons are as dangerous as their larger brethren, but different from them in two respects. The first is that their colour changes to a vivid blue, gaining them the name of Blue Horrors. The second is that the gleeful, moderately silly attitude of the Pink Horror is reversed, as all Blue Horrors are morose, whining and petty, eternally squabbling about whose fault it was that they lost their pink status again.

Some Pink Horrors are more powerful than their peers, and in the case of such deeply magical beings, greater power corresponds to a superior knowledge of their Master's Great Art. Some Horrors have the ability of reshaping their bodies to produce icons that act as a focus for the energies of the Warp. Others can mimic weird musical instruments, which accompany the Horrors' dissonant singing and invest it with an uncanny power over mortal minds. However, the most intelligent, independent and skilled amongst the Pink Horrors are the Heralds of Tzeentch, which can use their sorcery forcefully enough to blast any opponent into oblivion, or subtly enough to weave the most cunning of illusions.

	WS	BS	S	T	W	I	A	Ld	Sv
Pink Horror	2	3	3	3	1	3	1	10	4+
Herald of Tzeentch	2	4	3	3	2	4	2	10	4+

Unit Type:
Infantry.

Daemonic Gifts:
Pink Horrors have Warpfire.
Heralds have Daemonic Gaze instead.

Special Rules:
Daemon. Heralds are also Independent Characters.

Note on Blue Horrors:
For the sake of players' sanity, Pink Horrors splitting into two Blue Horrors is not represented in the rules. Players should feel free to mount two Blue Horror models on a single 25mm round base and mix them in their units for extra variety. These are treated exactly the same as a single Pink Horror.

> Where once was one, now there is two.
> Where once was pink, now there is blue.
>
> *From the Canticle of Change*

FLESH HOUNDS OF KHORNE
IMPLACABLE HUNTERS OF SOULS

The Hounds of Khorne are savage beasts that relentlessly hunt down the enemies of the Blood God. Once the Flesh Hounds have found the scent of the prey, nothing will stop them in their implacable chase, their bone-chilling howls the last sound their doomed quarry hears.

In the realm of Khorne, the Flesh Hounds are a threat to all creatures. Even Bloodthirsters must tread warily when out on the plains of powdered bone, for on their home territory the Flesh Hounds hunt in packs hundreds-strong. Occasionally a Juggernaut will break out of its pen and the Flesh Hounds will pounce on this rare prey – resulting in a titanic, prolonged battle as the Flesh Hounds circle their victim, while the Juggernaut charges and gores everything within reach of its tusks and hooves.

Many great heroes have offended Khorne, only to be implacably hunted throughout the galaxy by his mastiffs and then invariably caught, overpowered and dragged screaming back to the base of the Skull Throne. There, at a single word from their dark master, the Flesh Hounds tear their victims to pieces and scatter their bones, adding them to the huge collection that festoons the Brass Citadel of Khorne.

With steel-hard fangs the length of a dagger, powered by uncannily strong jaws, a red skin as tough as mesh armour and razor-sharp claws, the Flesh Hounds are a terrible foe for any mortal warrior. However, what makes them even more terrifying to the enemies of Khorne is the amazing speed that these feral Daemons can reach in a charge, their great limbs pushing them harder and faster towards their chosen victims.

One of the most recognisable features of the Flesh Hounds is the large iron and brass collar that seems to grow out of their thick necks. These are a boon from Khorne himself, not only physically protecting them against enemy blows, but also offering them a mystical ward against spells and other psychic attacks. This anti-psychic defence makes the Flesh Hounds the bane of all mortal servants of Tzeentch, and there is not one sorcerer in the galaxy that does not fear the Hunters of the Blood God.

Often the Hounds are conjured to the battlefield by the Overlord of a daemonic Legion, then sent to track down and slaughter the enemy commander or another target that is well hidden. Their packs are normally led by a larger Hound, a slavering beast of incomparable ferocity that has survived centuries of fights for supremacy in the pack.

	WS	BS	S	T	W	I	A	Ld	Sv
Flesh Hound	4	0	4	4	1	4	2	10	5+

Unit Type:
Beasts.

Daemonic Gifts:
Blessing of the Blood God.

Special Rules:
Daemon, Furious Charge.

> "First I heard the howling in my sleep, when I still could afford to rest, but now I hear it in my wake, continuous, growing ever louder as they get nearer. I have been running for weeks, but now I'm tired, so tired, and the Hounds are almost upon me."
>
> *Last record in the log of librarian Agapemachus*
> *before his disappearance.*

FIENDS OF SLAANESH
HARBINGERS OF DEADLY FRAGRANCE

Slaanesh's Fiends are Warp-birthed monstrosities drawn from narcotic-induced nightmares. They are chymerical hybrids of man, reptile and insect, given a single body by the perversity of the Dark Prince. A Fiend has a long, segmented body covered in delicate scales that shimmer as it moves. Its tail whips in serpentine coils, distracting and mesmerising in its movements. It has four legs ending in disturbingly humanoid feet, and two slender arms with vicious clamp-like claws that the Fiend uses to disembowel the enemy.

A Fiend's head is elongated and faintly bovine, with its multi-faceted eyes set far apart and its ears prominent and attentive. Its mouth is quite narrow but filled with sharp fangs between which a lithe, narrow tongue endlessly flickers, tasting the air for the scent of the Fiend's victims. This tongue contains a soporific poison that numbs the mind and body of those licked by a Fiend, causing them to fall into a coma during which the Fiends will slice them apart with luxurious slowness. A Fiend's head is crowned with gnarled horns, often asymmetrical in shape or contorted into one of the dark runes of Chaos.

Fiends move incredibly swiftly, skittering and leaping with unnatural agility towards their prey, using their pincers and tail to maintain their balance. Their bodies undulate in a sinuous manner as they run, having the appearance of a wafting breeze given physical form. As it sprints forward, a Fiend irregularly sashays from side-to-side, so that at times it appears to be running sideways or backwards, confounding the aim of the enemy.

As the Fiends gather for the kill, they let out a keening song to each other; a haunting discordance interweaved with melodic riffs and a throbbing, bass beat. This call is not merely sonic, but also psychic, resonating in Warpspace all the way back to the Palace of Pleasure. Slaanesh sprawls across his throne at times, his mind caught by the distant hymns and lullabies of the Fiends, his eyes glazed with the disturbing beauty of their music. For mortals, the call of the Fiends is less pleasurable, for the rapidly shifting scale and pitch can cause organs to fail, eyes to vitrify, ears to bleed and brains to burst. And even those warriors who are strong enough to survive this will soon be torn to shreds by the sharp claws of the charging Fiends.

When not fighting in Slaanesh's battles, the Fiends wander and prowl the circles of Slaanesh's realm, frolicking in the ever-present warm glow of Slaanesh's adoration. They amuse themselves by hunting each other and interlopers through the winding forests and along the beautiful shores. Attacking and then withdrawing, the Fiends carefully dissect their prey with precise cuts from their claws, toying for an age with those they chase until the final deathblow comes as an ecstatic release to their victim's agony.

	WS	BS	S	T	W	I	A	Ld	Sv
Fiend	4	0	5	4	2	5	5	10	5+

Unit Type:
Beasts.

Daemonic Gifts:
Soporific Musk, Rending Claws.

Special Rules:
Daemon.

"These creatures have no place in the Emperor's galaxy. Their unholy forms are an insult to reason and truth. Their impure songs will lead you to eternal damnation. Hell exists, and it sprang from the nightmares of mortals."

Inquisitor Thrax

BEASTS OF NURGLE
SLITHERING VESSELS OF CONTAGION

The Beasts of Nurgle are the embodiment of their creator's boundless enthusiasm and revel in the joy of decay. Leaving a foul trail of abominable slime behind them, they slither excitedly across the battlefield, eager to lavish affection on others and receive their loving attention in return. They often accompany the Plaguebearers, gurgling mirthfully as they bounce back and forth to attract the attention of Father Nurgle's favourite sons, hoping for a pat on the back or a rub of the belly. The Beasts of Nurgle are incarnations of the Plague Lord's own bountiful excitement, in turn a manifestation of all mortals' desire for energetic life, social interaction, affection and fertile endeavour.

This terrifying enthusiasm is made all the more nightmarish by the Beast of Nurgle's appearance. They are gigantic, slug-like creatures propelled forward with undulating ripples and clawed flippers. They have wide maws lined with rows of needle-like teeth, and bulging, excited eyes that drip with filthy lacrimation. Fronds of writhing tentacles sprout from their blob-like heads and along their back. Each is a waving tube of foulness that expels clouds of vomit-inducing gasses, clouds of flies and squirts of sour fluids that can seep through any armour and digest the tissues underneath.

It is these poisonous tentacles that a Beast of Nurgle wraps so affectionately around a newly-found playmate. Lavishing slobbery, deadly kisses from these waving members, the beast overwhelms its target with its great bulk and with its paralysing ichor and poisonous fumes. Soon the victim succumbs to this deadly assault and falls silent and still, quickly decaying under the influence of Nurgle's poxes. The Beast of Nurgle, disappointed by its new friend's lack of spirit, will quickly grow bored of its game and will leap onwards, searching for a new subject upon which to lavish its lethal devotion.

NURGLE'S ROT

Chief among the many gifts that Father Nurgle has granted an ungrateful galaxy is Nurgle's Rot. It is his masterpiece – completely incurable, highly infectious and with a very, very slow course. These characteristics allow it to spread uncontrollably, overwhelming whole continents, planets and star systems.

And that is not all. This perfect illness does not kill its host quickly, rather it slowly turns the victim's body into a bloated, rotting, living corpse. At the same time it erodes the victim's soul. It painfully corrupts it to the point where the tortured victim has to choose between the only two routes left open to him. He can either end his own life, or he can fully embrace the ways of Father Nurgle, dilecting in contagion and putrescence, revelling in buboes and sickness until death puts an end to his suffering.

Only then will he realise the true blessing that has been visited upon him, as his soul is reborn in Nurgle's realm, in the immortal shape of a new Plaguebearer.

	WS	BS	S	T	W	I	A	Ld	Sv
Beast	3	0	4	5	2	2	D6	10	5+

Unit Type:
Infantry.

Special Rules:
Daemon, Slow & Purposeful, Feel No Pain.

Random Poisoned Attacks. In close combat each Beast has D6 Attacks – roll every time they are about to attack. These attacks are poisoned (wounding on 4+, as described in the Warhammer 40,000 rulebook).

FLAMERS OF TZEENTCH
BEARERS OF THE TRUE FIRE OF CHANGE

The Pyrodaemons of Tzeentch, Keepers of the True Flame of Change, Candelabra Mutationi; many are the appellatives of these Daemons, but they all agree in describing their fiery nature. The body of a Flamer of Tzeentch looks deceptively slow and unwieldy, a headless conical torso to which are attached two long arms. These terminate in weird stumps, which are adorned with razor-sharp teeth and flickering tongues, and continuously belch out an acrid and sulphurous iridescent smoke.

Flamers move by bumping and hopping around, leaping high in the air in a disturbing and unnatural gravity-defying fashion, which may even appear amusing to the unknowing observer. Laughter soon turns to panic though, as the Flamers suddenly close in at unexpected speed and unleash roaring gouts of alchemical fire from their arms, incinerating anything in their path.

Of course their flames are nothing like the fire mortals have experienced on their own worlds, where the laws of nature apply. The effects of the Fire of Change are as unpredictable as they are devastating – sometimes burning metal, flesh and stone equally to ashes in a multi-hued conflagration, sometimes turning to frozen crystal anything they come into contact with, while in other cases they might just spray the surprised enemies with an iridescent cascade of sweet-tasting liquor. They have been known to project lethal gasses that dissolve all living tissues, leaving behind only empty armour and uniforms, while on other occasions they have exactly the opposite effect, leaving the victims untouched, but naked, unarmed and defenceless in the middle of the battlefield. Episodes like this never fail to cause great bouts of uncontrollable laughter and much clapping and cheering from all Pink Horrors that witness them.

Flamers make perfect troops to lead assaults against defensive positions, as there is no fortification that can offer protection against their magical vapours. Much like other Daemons of Tzeentch, the Flamers do not excel at close quarters, preferring to engage their enemies at range. Also, just like the Pink Horrors, they are extremely difficult to destroy because of their absurd physiologies, which have no obvious vital points for an enemy to aim for.

	WS	BS	S	T	W	I	A	Ld	Sv
Flamer	2	4	4	4	1	3	2	10	4+

Unit Type:
Jump Infantry.

Daemonic Gifts:
Warpfire, Breath of Chaos.

Special Rules:
Daemon.

"Don't you see? My Master Tzeentch cares not which of the Great Powers of Chaos you serve.

In the end, aren't the followers of the Blood God changing valiant warriors into headless corpses? Aren't the worshippers of the Lord of Flies changing strong, healthy bodies into rotting, diseased carcasses? Aren't the disciples of the Dark Prince changing stern, steadfast heroes into slaves to their own senses?

Chaos is a struggle to change, you must agree. Change rules all."

Amon 'Chakai to the Rathelian Congregation

BLOODCRUSHERS
BRASS KNIGHTS OF KHORNE

Juggernauts of Khorne are large daemonic creatures that inhabit the realm of the Blood God. These dim-witted brutes are covered in solid metal plates and have mechanical elements in their bodies, testament to the part that the armourers and weapon-smiths of Khorne have in their creation.

Juggernauts are slow, but nigh unstoppable, and their charging bulk can ram into most enemy vehicles and send them flying, or flatten squad after squad of mortal warriors. The puny small arms fire of enemy infantry patters harmlessly from a Juggernaut's impenetrable hide and it only makes the beast even more intractable and violent. Only anti-tank weapons have a realistic chance of penetrating its armour and stopping its rampaging mass.

The strongest warriors amongst the legions of the Bloodletters, together with some of Khorne's Heralds and a few of the mortal champions of the Blood God, ride Juggernauts into battle. Such an undertaking is not for the cowardly, for a Bloodletter must dare the corral where the Juggernauts are kept, to choose his mount. Once dragged forth from its stable, at first the beast is as dangerous for its rider as it is for the enemy, but once mastered a Juggernaut becomes the most lethal of all war-mounts.

These daemonic knights are known as Bloodcrushers, and are capable of the most murderous charges. They trample the enemy underfoot like an unstoppable tide, the ground shaking under their heavy tread. Horns gashing and gutting the fallen, Hellblades slashing down in great arcs to behead the few enemies still standing, this rampaging wall of steel and brass is a nightmare that even the bravest of warriors pray they will never have to face on a battlefield, lest their courage fail them.

	WS	BS	S	T	W	I	A	Ld	Sv
Bloodcrusher	5	0	5	5	2	4	3	10	5+

Unit Type:
Infantry (as they are too slow to be treated as cavalry).

Daemonic Gifts:
Hellblades, Iron Hide.

Special Rules:
Daemon, Furious Charge.

Note: *Bloodcrushers are Bloodletters mounted on Juggernauts, but Heralds of Khorne can ride Juggernauts too (see 'Daemonic Steeds' on page 76).*

LORD OF THE SLAUGHTER

According to the whim of Khorne, the Daemons of his realm take part in an immense tournament. Khorne takes the Daemonsword known as Khartoth the Bloodhunger, which is capable of cutting through not only matter but also time, and hides it within one of his Flesh Hounds. The legions of Khorne fall upon each other with sword and axe, slaughtering and butchering whilst hunting the Flesh Hounds, who tear apart any Daemon who approaches. The Daemon brave, strong or fortunate enough to slay the Flesh Hound containing the Daemonsword becomes the Lord of the Slaughter and may wield the Bloodhunger. For a day or an age, as Khorne sees fit, the Lord of the Slaughter enjoys great privilege in battle. When Khorne wearies of his Lord of the Slaughter's exploits, the Blood God begins the tournament again. A Flesh Hound devours both wielder and sword, combining their essence, and the Daemons battle again until Khorne finds a new Lord of the Slaughter.

SEEKERS
SWIFT RIDERS OF SLAANESH

Hidden deep within the circles of Slaanesh's realm are great meadows of gold and silver that crest into rolling hills and idyllic dales. Here roam the herds of the Mounts of Slaanesh, hundreds of them gathered in large groups running freely across the iridescent plains. They are incarnations of Slaanesh's free spirit, allowed to flit and run where they please. Like birds on the wing, they migrate across the magical pastures, suddenly altering direction en masse as some whim takes them, shifting colour from soft blues to pastel purples and gentle ochres.

A Mount of Slaanesh is a swift and powerful creature, with a serpentine body propelled on two long, muscular legs. Its head is extremely narrow, little more than a slender snout with eyes, from which a tongue several metres long flicks and darts. With this tongue the Steed of Slaanesh can taste the desire of mortals, following its scent for many miles. They have glittering eyes that seem full of loving intelligence, yet the Mounts of Slaanesh are purely beasts, driven by the fancies of the Dark Prince and nothing else.

Sometimes a Daemonette or, rarer still, a mortal will steal into Slaanesh's sacred pastures to secure themselves a steed from amongst the herds. Such an endeavour is arduous, for the Mounts do not tire and can run for eternity, quickly outpacing any pursuer. To succeed, the hunter must be more wily, and exploit the insatiable curiosity of the creatures. Like all Daemons of Slaanesh, the Mounts crave experience, and they will quickly investigate something that is new or different. A cunning pursuer can lure a Mount with some shining gem or silvery bauble. Also, rivers made of mother's milk or scented oil flow through the pastures, and from these gentle streams the Mounts drink, lapping up the agony and ecstasy of Slaanesh. At these times the Mounts are distracted and vulnerable, and most likely to be caught.

If a Daemonette can sneak close to a Mount while it remains unaware of her, she can use a chain of fine gold or silver to ensnare it. Steeds are vicious when roused, their tongues lashing like whips, their clawed feet kicking and eviscerating. Once she has chained her steed, the Daemonette leaps upon its back and caresses its neck and flanks to calm its anger.

Once she has placated her mount, the Daemonette rides from the pasture and joins her fellow Daemons as a Seeker of Slaanesh, the Dark Prince's immortal huntresses. The Daemonette adorns her steed with sigils and runes, and harnesses it with tethers made of loyalty and worship. It is said that a Seeker can never let go of her Mount, for once free of her touch, it will escape her beguiling embrace and race to the magical meadows to frolic with its herd once again.

	WS	BS	S	T	W	I	A	Ld	Sv
Seeker	4	0	3	3	1	6	4	10	5+

Unit Type:
Cavalry.

Daemonic Gifts:
Aura of Acquiescence, Rending Claws.

Special Rules:
Daemon.

Note: Seekers are Daemonettes riding Mounts of Slaanesh, but Heralds of Slaanesh can ride these Mounts too (see 'Daemonic Steeds' on page 76).

> "This way sisters! There's the prey! I love it when they run."
>
> *Sheee'la'sar, leader of the hunt*

NURGLINGS
MITES OF FATHER NURGLE

The innards of a Great Unclean One are best left as imponderables by mortals, for such twisting gastric caverns and voluminous guts are not a place one wishes to consider for too long. It is in these dark, churning depths that the Nurglings are born. Starting as small blobs of indescribably foul matter, Nurglings are nourished by the pulsating juices of a Great Unclean One's inner organs, growing into small facsimiles of Nurgle himself. Once a Nurgling has matured, the peristaltic heavings of the Great Unclean One's internal processes will eventually deposit the Nurgling through some orifice or tear in the flesh, plopping them into existence as spiteful, rotund imps.

For most of their existence, Nurglings will congregate around the grand Daemon that birthed them. They clamber across his bulk seeking comfortable pools of liquids and warm spots under the folds of rolling flesh, constantly bickering in petty territorial war. Eager for the attention of their master, the Nurglings sit on the shoulders of the Great Unclean One and chatter to him incessantly, hoping for a fatherly pat or belch of appreciation. Other times they will scurry around the Greater Daemon making gifts of small trinkets they find; dead animals, rotting bones, particularly splendid fungi and other such presents as they think will please their master. Such a life is not without its risks, for in an absent-minded moment a Great Unclean One will sit or tread upon his tiny charges, or gulp down one or two as delicate sweetmeats.

When the Great Unclean One fights, the Nurglings leave their master and swarm forwards as a living carpet of malevolent pettiness. Possessed of pointed teeth and sharp claws, the Nurglings swallow up their enemies with a mound of biting, scratching bodies. Such small wounds as are inflicted by these tiny creatures would be inconsequential were it not for the lively toxins and diseases from which the Nurglings are made, which quickly infect and mortify even the slightest injury.

Sometimes a particularly well-favoured Herald of Nurgle is gifted a palanquin upon which to be carried. Sitting upon rotted boards atop a carpet of Nurglings, the Herald can look down upon all of the other Plaguebearers – figuratively as well as literally. The Nurglings are very protective of their passenger and will launch themselves at foes who threaten their charge, gurgling angrily, teeth and claws bared.

Perhaps of all Daemons, it is the Nurglings that most vex the Plaguebearers. Driven by the instinct to record and codify, Plaguebearers find the capricious, mischievous nature of the Nurglings impossible to fathom. While the Great Unclean Ones look upon their pestilent children with affection, the sombre Plaguebearers view them as a constant distraction.

	WS	BS	S	T	W	I	A	Ld	Sv
Nurglings	2	0	3	3	3	2	3	10	5+

Unit Type:
Infantry.

Special Rules:
Daemon, Swarm.

Note: Nurglings can also carry the Palanquin of a Herald of Nurgle (as explained in the 'Daemonic Steeds' rules on page 76).

"Sarge, what's that smell? Sarge? Saaarge!"

Private Roth of the Cadian 42nd

SCREAMERS
TZEENTCH'S SOARING PREDATORS

Screamers of Tzeentch are also known as Sky-sharks, due to their predatory behaviour. They hunt through the vast sea of the Immaterium in great packs, elegantly hovering on their outstretched membranous bodies. As they slice through the ether, they leave behind them multi-coloured, sparkling trails, and emit the high-pitched screeching sound that earns them their name.

Screamers are of limited intelligence when compared with most servants of the Great Schemer, but their animal instincts are tinged with a strong sense of cunning. They tend to use their great speed and manoeuvrability to surprise their prey and bring it down with a short-ranged burst of sorcerous lightning from their horns and tails.

Drawn by the presence of mortal souls, Screamers race through the Realm of Chaos seeking their prey. Vicious shoals of Screamers often follow ships in the Warp, patiently probing its psychic defences. Should a weakness be found, the Screamers stream through the gap in its shields and attack the hull. In the mortal realm, a tank's turret or Dreadnought's sarcophagus provides scant protection against jaws that can be used to prise open an armoured starship!

Tzeentch occasionally grants the use of a Screamer as a mount for one of his Heralds, or even for one of his mortal champions. In this case the Master of Change binds the Screamer with bands and blades of gold and silver, chaining it to the rider's will without losing any of its renowned speed. These bound Screamers are then known as Discs of Tzeentch. Since the dawn of time the arrival of a shining Herald, riding the surf of the cosmic currents on his mount, has spelled the doom of many a planet throughout the galaxy, announcing the intention of its maker and lord to feed upon the very essence of the world.

	WS	BS	S	T	W	I	A	Ld	Sv
Screamers	3	0	4	4	1	3	1	10	4+

Unit Type:
Jetbikes.

Special Rules:
Daemon.
Warp Jaws. Screamers count as equipped with melta bombs.

Note: Screamers can be changed by the Great Sorcerer into Discs of Tzeentch to provide mounts for his Heralds (see 'Daemonic Steeds' on page 76).

GELLAR FIELDS

In order to traverse the Warp, a starship must be enveloped in a protective bubble. Imperial ships create a skin of reality around their hulls with a device known as a Gellar field. The creation of Gellar field technology is a secret held closely by the Adeptus Mechanicus and Adeptus Astra Telepathica. The Gellar field projects a psychic ward against the energy of Warpspace, protecting the ship against the corruption of raw Chaos as well as daemonic attack. However, just as Daemons can break through into the mortal universe, they can also breach the defences of a Gellar field. Sometimes this begins with the possession of crew members, other times full physical manifestation of Daemons can overwhelm a ship. Such vessels are left to drift through Warpspace, and are deposited somewhere in space and time as sinister ghostships. Crews boarding them have often reported disembodied voices, strange shadows, beguiling lights long after the Daemons themselves have departed. For this reason, Imperial warships are under standing orders to destroy these ghostships on contact.

SOUL GRINDERS
IRON DOOMSTRIDERS OF CHAOS

In the Formless Wastes of the Realm of Chaos there is a place that is perpetually cloaked in a pall of black, oily fumes, rank with the acrid stench of forbidden metallurgy, dominated by a cacophony of strident grinding and the wailing of uncountable tortured spirits. This accursed place is known as the Forge of Souls, where the blind, ever-mutating Daemon craftsmen of Chaos eternally hammer at their creations in cyclopean smitheries.

The black fires of these cavernous laboratories are fuelled by the souls of the damned and kept roaring by colossal screaming bellows, manned by legions of semi-sentient nightmare creatures. From the dark bowels of the Forge of Souls come all manner of hideous and unholy weapons. By means of the perverse technologies of the artisans of Chaos, daemonic energies are fused with arcane metals to create great jagged blades, weeping swords, barbed steel whips and other potent weapons and talismans, to be used by the Daemons in their eternal warfare.

But as lethal as such weapons are, they are mere toys next to the greatest construct of the daemonic smiths – the dreaded Soul Grinders. These terrifying creatures are the fusion of the most powerful of daemonic entities with machines of war that originate from outside the Immaterium, but already have felt the touch of Chaos. These are often the wrecked remains of great Daemon engines and other possessed vehicles, like the mighty Battle Titans of the Legio Mortis, or the rampaging Defilers created by the Traitor Legions. All this ruined materiel is absorbed into the Warp as the flotsam and jetsam of a galaxy at war, flowing from real space into the Immaterium through the Eye of Terror, the Maelstrom and the other loci where different realities touch.

In the ash plains outside the Forge of Souls battle never stops, as many amongst the higher ranks of Daemonhood vie with each other and duel for the chance of being the one to fuse with the mechanical constructs and become a Soul Grinder. This is because, unlike a possessed mortal body, these steel and ceramite shells can sustain a Daemon in the mortal world for decades, even centuries. During this time, the shape of each Soul Grinder will change, as their metal body slowly becomes more similar to the Daemon possessing it.

Such a precious armoured form does not come for free. Great is the price that the artisans of the Forge invariably demand of each new Soul Grinder in return for the unholy incarnation. Before being released, the Daemon must take the three Oaths of the Iron Pact with the Masters of the Forge. First, that all of the souls harvested by the great blades of the Soul Grinder will be used for the fuelling of the Forge. Second, that the wrecked remains of all of the war machines destroyed by the adamantium claws of the Soul Grinder will be offered to the Forge. Finally, and perhaps most significantly, that should one of the Chaos Gods attack the Forge of Souls and try to rule over it, all Soul Grinders will fight in its defence, discarding all of their previous loyalties to any of the four Great Powers of Chaos.

In battle, Soul Grinders form the armoured spearhead of the daemonic hosts, using their massive firepower to hammer the enemy lines, covering the rank-and-file troops of the Dark Gods as they close in with the enemy. Their daemonic nature allows them to appear out of thin air where least expected, and their ceramite hull, animated and protected by the supernatural energies of the Immaterium, makes them invulnerable to small-arms fire and resilient to the hits of all but the most powerful anti-tank weapons. As they advance implacably towards the enemy, the Soul Grinders keep up a continuous barrage with their dreaded harvester guns, rapid-firing weapons built by the artisans of Chaos from the vestiges of ancient weaponry from the world of mortals.

But those are not the most powerful weapons in a Soul Grinder's arsenal – its smoking maw is capable of unleashing the baleful energies of the Warp itself against the enemy. These attacks can take many different forms, all as lethal as they are bizarre to the eyes of mortal warriors. Sometimes the Soul Grinders can vomit great gouts of Warpflame, while at other times their tongue-like appendage lashes out like a searing energy ray. They have even been known to spit huge roiling masses of mutating ichor at incredible distances, annihilating entire enemy squads in one great blast. At close quarters all Soul Grinders are unstoppable – great metal behemoths whose many limbs are armed with piston-powered crushing claws and daemonic weapons crackling with unearthly powers. The brutal impetus and indomitable violence of their assaults are so horrifying that very few warriors have a chance of fighting back, or even standing their ground when a Soul Grinder storms their lines.

	Range	Strength	AP	Type
Vomit	Template	6	4	Assault 1
Tongue	24"	10	1	Assault 1
Phlegm	36"	8	3	Assault 1, Large Blast

Armour									
	WS	BS	S	F	S	R	I	A	
Soul Grinder	3	3	6	13	13	11	3	4	

Unit Type:
Vehicle (Walker)

Special Rules:
Fleet, Daemon (for Soul Grinders this rule simply means they deploy like all other Daemons, and are immune to the 'Shaken' and 'Stunned' damage results).

Weapons:
Mawcannon: Soul Grinders can unleash lethal Warp energies from their mouth. All Soul Grinders can use their Mawcannon with the Vomit profile shown below, but only some are powerful enough to use the Tongue or the Phlegm profiles. This is represented by upgrades that can be bought for the model in the army list. If these upgrades are purchased, the cannon can then be fired as any of the profiles available (the player must declare before firing it). A 'weapon destroyed' result on the cannon destroys all profiles.

Harvester: As well as the dreaded Mawcannon, Soul Grinders are gifted with Harvester guns, which have the following profile:

	Range	Strength	AP	Type
Harvester	24"	4	5	Assault 6

All of the souls you will reap.
All of your spoils of war.
To be a keeper of the Forge.
But a trifle price for the boon that is bestowed upon you.

From the Iron Pact

As the Space Marines rushed through the battle barge's corridors towards the reported position of the breach, they could hear the blasts and explosions of a protracted firefight. They eventually reached a sealed bulkhead, which barred their progress, emergency lights flashing intermittently, a strong sulphuric stench filling the air.

Through the reinforced steel the sounds of battle continued for a few seconds, only to be abruptly replaced by an ominous silence. A rhythmic noise reached them from the other side, like the sound of heavy steps approaching the massive gate. Then all was silence once again. And suddenly it happened.

The bulkhead exploded inwards with a cataclysmic crash, and a colossus out of a nightmare – part machine, part daemon – stormed into the corridor. The thing was totally oblivious to the bolter shells that met its entrance. White-hot warpflame erupted from his maw and engulfed the Space Marines, instantly turning some of the armoured warriors into a cloud of ashes.

Priming a hand grenade, the Brother-Sergeant led his men in a desperate charge against the mechanical Daemon. The ensuing melee was pitifully uneven and extremely short. The mighty steel claws of the beast easily crushed the impotent Space Marines, tossing their remains aside in a spray of gore. Lastly, the Soul Grinder picked up the struggling Sergeant and, taking hold of each of the Space Marine's limbs in a vice-strong grip, the behemoth slowly quartered him.

The Soul Grinder briefly inspected the scene of carnage, looking for more souls to reap and finally, disappointed, it moved on in search of more prey.

DAEMON PRINCES
IMMORTAL CHAMPIONS

Very rarely a mortal Champion of Chaos manages to earn the ultimate reward for his deeds and unbending loyalty to one of the Dark Gods – immortality. The Champion becomes a Daemon Prince, a great asset to the Dark Gods, with powers that rival those of the Greater Daemons. Some Daemon Princes discard their material form altogether and join the ranks of their patron's Daemons, coming back to haunt the galaxy as part of a daemonic invasion, in the shape of large and unstoppable daemonic creatures. These Daemon Princes often act as lieutenants to the Greater Daemons – powerful warriors and forceful leaders capable of fighting at the forefront of a daemonic assault. However, other Daemons consider Daemon Princes to be inferior – deeply and irrevocably tainted by their mortal origins.

	WS	BS	S	T	W	I	A	Ld	Sv
Daemon Prince	7	5	5	5	4	5	4	10	5+

Unit Type:
Monstrous Creature

Special Rules:
Daemon

FURIES OF CHAOS
SLAVES TO DARKNESS

It has been conjectured that the Furies are made of the souls of mortals that could never decide which of the Gods of Chaos to serve – not because of a genuine love for all four of them, but from a continuous swaying from the worship of one Chaos God to another, driven only by the prospect of personal gain. When their souls are finally released from their mortal husks, no Power claims them – their tragic fate is to be forbidden from entering any of their Realms. Instead, they spend eternity in the shape of a grotesque gargoyle, condemned to be buffeted by the whimsical currents of the Immaterium, with no direction and no meaning, forever. Such is the destiny of the indecisive.

When a Daemonic Legion breaks into reality, these bestial Daemons see their opportunity of a temporary respite from their eternal torture, and flock onto the battlefield to vent their impotent anger against some unfortunate mortal.

	WS	BS	S	T	W	I	A	Ld	Sv
Fury	3	0	4	4	1	3	2	10	5+

Unit Type:
Jump Infantry

Special Rules:
Daemon

SKARBRAND
THE EXILED ONE

No Daemon lord of Khorne ever served the Blood God more faithfully and shed blood more enthusiastically than Skarbrand. This Bloodthirster led the greatest of Khorne's armies and slaughtered untold millions in the cause of carnage. Skarbrand left worlds desolated in his wake and ravaged the realms of the other gods with equal rage. It was this utter dedication to destruction that proved to be Skarbrand's undoing.

Tzeentch noted the prowess of Khorne's favoured slaughterer and with whispers fuelled Skarbrand's anger. With constant taunting Tzeentch goaded Skarbrand into ever greater acts of bloodletting, until Skarbrand was a burning figure of incandescent fury. So great did Skarbrand's rage grow that when Khorne's attention was elsewhere Skarbrand took up his axe and struck a blow against the Blood God.

Though powerful enough to have felled an army, Skarbrand's strike only opened a small chink in the armour of the Blood God and attracted the desolate gaze of Khorne. Filled with an anger that made Skarbrand's own rage seem meek, Khorne snatched up the wayward Bloodthirster in his clawed grip. Bellowing damning curses, Khorne choked Skarbrand until all vestige of personality and thought had been driven out, leaving only the flaming ire that had powered that fateful axe stroke. Khorne dragged Skarbrand to the pinnacle of the Brass Citadel and held aloft the Bloodthirster for all to see. As an example to all who dared challenge the Blood God's might, Khorne hurled Skarbrand across the Realms of Chaos.

For eight days and nights Skarbrand blazed a trail of fiery destruction across the realms of the gods, leaving a scorched waste in his wake. As a rage-filled meteor, he plunged down, carving a great canyon with his landing, his wings torn to shreds by the force of the impact. Exiled and consumed by frustration, Skarbrand bellowed his wrath and set upon an eternity of slaughter that would dwarf all the bloodshed that had come before.

Roused only by the anger that spurred his mindless betrayal, Skarbrand has become the incarnation of mindless wrath. His being exudes anarchy and death, and where he treads bloodshed and war follow. No loyalty or logic can defy Skarbrand's aura of destruction. No alliance is bond against the bloodshed caused by Skarbrand. No cowardice survives the overwhelming need to slay inspired by Skarbrand.

Driven on by his geas of obliteration, Skarbrand and his two legendary Daemon-axes have shed oceans of blood in the name of Khorne. It is all for nothing, as Khorne has no mercy in his heart, and the Bloodthirster's exile is eternal. In tortured banishment, Skarbrand serves his lord more wholly than ever.

	WS	BS	S	T	W	I	A	Ld	Sv
Skarbrand	10	0	8	6	4	5	6	10	4+

Unit Type:
Monstrous Creature.

Daemonic Gifts:
Iron Hide.

Special Rules:
Daemon, Fleet, Furious Charge.

Rage Embodied: The presence of Skarbrand infects all warriors on the battlefield with the deepest bloodlust. Skarbrand and every unit within 24" of the Exiled One (friend and foe alike!) must re-roll failed rolls to hit in close combat.

Bellow of Endless Fury: To represent the devastating effects of Skarbrand's battle roar, he has the Breath of Chaos and Instrument of Chaos daemonic gifts.

KU'GATH
THE PLAGUEFATHER

Ku'gath was once a Nurgling, a mite upon the great shoulders of Nurgle. Whilst the Lord of Decay mixed his most virulent toxin ever, Ku'gath tumbled from his nesting place into the cauldron. Ku'gath took a great draught of the filthy contents of that rusted bowl and swelled with its power. Invigorated, he drank and drank and drank until the cauldron was empty. As he filled with the corrupting power of decay, Ku'gath grew into a mighty Great Unclean One. Nurgle laughed at the antics of his new creation, who had become the embodiment of the perfect disease that had bubbled in the cauldron of poxes. Though Nurgle was unperturbed by the turn of events, Ku'gath realised he had robbed his father of the greatest of all diseases. Ever since, Ku'gath has sought to recreate the toxic miracle that created him.

He is a sombre creature, standing apart from his fellow Greater Daemons. Not for Ku'gath the gurgling delights of infection. Ku'gath is studious and observant, the better to create the perfect disease. Ku'gath has travelled widely, seeking every ingredient and sickness imaginable. Atop a palanquin carried under a mound of straining Nurglings, Ku'gath moves across the

universes searching for the combination of blights and woes that will create his perfect disease. As well as the considerable bulk of Ku'gath, the palanquin is loaded with the paraphernalia of Ku'gath's mobile laboratory. Burning braziers heat warped alembics that bubble with corroding fumes. Rusted pipes funnel bacteria through fungal sieves, distilling poisons procured from a thousand million worlds and the furthest reaches of the ever-changing Realms of Chaos.

Ku'gath uses war to conduct his field tests, unleashing clouds of spores and bacteria that wipe out whole armies. The Nurglings that grow from within Ku'gath each carry a unique blend of the elements that created the Great Unclean One. He hurls his pestilent Nurglings at his enemies, watching with detached interest as the symptoms of each particular infection begin to spread. Ku'gath also captures those his diseases corrupt, taking them back to his ruinous lair in the manse of Nurgle where he can observe their degeneration more closely. In thousands of cages that stretch into the darkness, creatures of every single species from all across time and space gibber, wail and moan in the gloom.

	WS	BS	S	T	W	I	A	Ld	Sv
Ku'gath	6	4	6	6	6	2	5	10	4+

Unit Type:
Monstrous Creature.

Daemonic Gifts:
Cloud of Flies, Noxious Touch, Breath of Chaos, Aura of Decay.

Special Rules:
Daemon, Slow & Purposeful, Feel no Pain.

Necrotic Missiles: Ku'gath can scoop up and lob against the enemy vast handfuls of Nurglings filled with the most devastating concoctions of the Plaguefather. This is treated as a ranged poisoned weapon (wounding on a 4+) with the following profile:

Range	Strength	AP	Type
24"	n/a	2	Ordnance 1, Large Blast

Nurgling Infestation: At the beginning of any turn in which Ku'gath is on the table (not including the one when he arrives from Reserve), the player may roll a dice on behalf of the Plaguefather. On a roll of 4+, a new unit consisting of a single base of Nurglings enters the game by Deep Strike within 12" of Ku'gath.

FATEWEAVER
THE ORACLE OF TZEENTCH

Tzeentch's gaze encompasses all of the past and all of the present. The future, however, is a different matter. There are infinite futures, fragmented into uncountable threads, ever changing, ever twisting. Events in the present generate a new thread, which instantly intertwines millions of others, created by the actions of creatures in all corners of the universe. Not even the Great Sorcerer can hold all of the threads in his mighty intellect. This limit has always unnerved Tzeentch. The need to overcome this one weakness took the Lord of Mutation to the very centre of reality, to the mystic Well of Eternity, where space and time originate and end. But even Tzeentch himself was afraid of entering the Well. Instead, he sent his most powerful and trusted Greater Daemons, but none of the Lords of Change ever returned from the roiling currents of the Well.

Exasperated, Tzeentch grabbed his vizir, Kairos, the first among his Greater Daemons, and cast him into the Well. To Tzeentch's delight, the Daemon survived, just. When Kairos resurfaced, his body was now hunched and wizened, unnaturally aged for such an immortal creature. His mighty pinions were reduced to feeble vestigial remains. The strangest change was that Kairos's head and neck had split along their length and now the vizir had two separate heads, which shared both the knowledge of the future and the resulting insanity. Now Kairos sits on Tzeentch's right as his Oracle, mumbling madly and suddenly bursting into rambling tirades about events still to happen. Nine times nine Lords of Change are tasked with recording every word of the Oracle, every fragment of mysterious knowledge.

A few mighty individuals, Daemon and mortal alike, are granted an audience with the Oracle as a reward for the completion of the most challenging of quests for the Lord of Mutation. This is a great boon indeed, for the Oracle knows the answer to all questions and one of the two heads will always answer the truth. Sadly, the other head simultaneously delivers a contradictory answer, false but equally believable. The resulting riddle leaves the petitioner invariably baffled, and often in total despair.

On rare occasions Tzeentch sends the Oracle to a battlefield in the mortal world, where Kairos is known as Fateweaver. There the Oracle uses his great magical powers and infallible prescience to influence the course of the battle. Torrents of warping energy are unleashed upon the enemy, twisting and changing the very battlefield. Mortal warriors shoot and slash in vain against Fateweaver and his daemonic bodyguard, foes that know exactly how to move in order not to be hit before the gun is fired or the blade is drawn. This gift, however, has a critical consequence: if any unexpected harm comes to him, Fateweaver often retreats back to the Warp, afraid that his treacherous Master might have intentionally concealed that future from him.

	WS	BS	S	T	W	I	A	Ld	Sv
Fateweaver	4	5	5	5	3	4	2	9	3+

Unit Type:
Monstrous Creature.

Daemonic Gifts:
Daemonic Flight, Master of Sorcery, We are Legion, Soul Devourer, Bolt of Tzeentch, Boon of Mutation, Daemonic Gaze, Breath of Chaos.

Special Rules:
Daemon.

Oracle of Eternity:
Because of the incredible prescience of the Oracle of Tzeentch, Fateweaver and all friendly units within 6" may re-roll all failed Armour, Invulnerable and Cover saves. However, for every unsaved wound suffered by Fateweaver, take a Ld test. If the test is failed, he retreats in shock and is removed as a casualty.

SKULLTAKER
THE CHAMPION OF KHORNE

It is said that when Khorne first created the Daemon U'Zuhl, the Bloodletter's first act was to chop the head from the first creature he met – another Bloodletter. So began an existence of decapitation that has spread terror throughout the mortal and immortal universes. When U'zuhl took his eight hundred and eighty-eighth skull, Khorne anointed him as his Sacred Executioner and U'Zuhl earned the title of Skulltaker.

In the middle of the greatest slaughter, whether against the hordes of the other gods, amongst his own kind or when ravaging a world of mortals, Skulltaker always seeks out the mightiest of the enemy's warriors. He fought alongside the Primarch Angron on Armageddon felling a quarter of the Grey Knights Brother-Captains. On Agripina-6 Skulltaker slew the Ork Grimsnag Urk after butchering the Warlord's armoured bodyguard. Seventeen Eldar Exarchs fell to his blade during the fighting at Haranshemash. Every race has its legends concerning the Skulltaker, and all are filled with terror.

He is a fearsome sight mounted atop a great Juggernaut, his wickedly serrated blade in hand. Skulltaker hacks his way through the fray so that he may confront his chosen opponent and offer them the rites of single combat. Those that flee are cut down without thought, not worthy of any greater ceremony; those that foolishly stand and fight suffer a slower death.

A duellist beyond compare, Skulltaker weaves his blade in bloody crescents that dismember and despoil but do not slay. Only when his foe is limbless upon the ground does Skulltaker offer them final release. He grasps their head in his hand and, uttering the eight Words of Sacrifice, he wreathes his victim's head in magical flames, blistering away all skin and flesh until only bare skull remains. With a savage twist, he tears free the naked skull, snapping it from the spine and holding it aloft for all to see. After a wrathful glare, Skulltaker places his prize in the great sack he carries upon his back, alongside the other skull-trophies taken in that battle. He then carves his way towards his next victim and proceeds to enact the same ritual, over and over until no foe worthy of such treatment remains.

When he returns to the Brass Citadel, Skulltaker presents his new trophies to his master. Most Khorne takes for himself having them impaled upon brass spikes that adorn the ramparts of his keep. A few, those that offered a real challenge, Khorne allows Skulltaker to keep. U'Zuhl weaves these into his cloak using bloody sinew, to sit alongside his other great triumphs. Soon his bloodthirst stirs again, and Skulltaker mounts his Juggernaut and rides off to find his next opponent.

	WS	BS	S	T	W	I	A	Ld	Sv
Skulltaker	7	3	4	4	2	5	4	10	5+
Skulltaker on Juggernaut	7	3	5	5	3	5	5	10	5+
Skulltaker on Chariot	7	3	5	5	4	5	5	10	5+

Unit Type:
Infantry.

Daemonic Gifts:
Hellblade, Fury of Khorne, Blessing of the Blood God, Iron Hide.

Special Rules:
Daemon, Furious Charge, Independent Character.

Skulls for the Skull Throne! Against non-vehicle models, Skulltaker's close combat attacks are Rending on rolls of 4+ instead of 6, and any of his Rending wounds also inflicts Instant Death (chop!).

THE MASQUE
ETERNAL DANCER OF SLAANESH

Once the chief handmaiden of Slaanesh, it was the Masque that combed the Dark Prince's shining hair and oiled it with fragrant balms. When Slaanesh's mood was grim, the Masque would dance to lighten his thoughts, enrapturing her god with the most dazzling and acrobatic displays. Yet for all of Slaanesh's indulgence, the Masque was to become the most despised of all the Prince of Pleasure's servants.

During the eternal wrangling and wars that make up the Great Game, it came about that Tzeentch tricked Slaanesh into battling with Khorne. The Changer of Ways lured Slaanesh into a cause he could not hope to achieve, and Slaanesh was defeated and humiliated. Seeing the dark mood of her master, the Masque took it upon herself to ease his heart with her most energetic and scintillating dance ever. Where once her leaps and pirouettes had brought laughter and joy, now Slaanesh's bitter heart saw mockery, each perfect combination of moves calculated to be barbs into his pierced pride. Slaanesh cast the Masque aside, condemning her as a traitor. He cursed her, saying that if she wanted to dance, she must dance forever more.

Such has been the Masque's doom, to dance across eternity. In the circles of Slaanesh's realm she dances for other Daemonettes, entrancing them with her sinuous movements until they are so enraptured they can no longer move or speak. She dances at the gates of Khorne, mocking the Bloodletters who snarl and growl at her impudence. The Masque dances across the mortal worlds of the galaxy, trapping those who witness her. Where mortals indulge their senses, where excess overcomes restraint, the Masque appears to lead the incautious on a dance of doom. As she enacts the tales of Slaanesh's greatest victories and most unholy conquests, her golden mask flickers and changes, matching the roles of the characters she plays. So powerful is the lure of the Masque's display that all who see it feel compelled to join in the performance. Immortal Daemons and crude mortals alike feel this calling in their hearts and are powerless to resist. As the dance goes on, the tempo rises, while the Masque's unwitting chorus leap and flail in their attempts to keep up. Consumed by the ecstasy and agony of the Masque's aura, they dance themselves to death, using up their last ounce of energy, their dying breath, to keep pace with her twirls and somersaults.

No-one knows the Masque better than the Harlequins. They have a performance that tells the tale of how the Masque once infiltrated one of their troupes. As the Harlequins and their audience were drawn into the Masque's whirling spell, a Solitaire appeared. The only Harlequin able to perform the role of Slaanesh in the Great Dance, the Solitaire matched the Masque move for move, and for six days and nights they cavorted and whirled, until the Masque finally faltered and missed a step. Horrified, she fled on sparkling feet and now seeks revenge on the followers of the Laughing God.

	WS	BS	S	T	W	I	A	Ld	Sv
The Masque	5	4	3	3	2	7	4	10	3+

Unit Type:
Infantry.

Daemonic Gifts:
Rending Claws, We are Legion, Instrument of Chaos, Pavane of Slaanesh, Aura of Acquiescence, Soporific Musk.

Special Rules:
Daemon, Fleet.

Eternal Dance: To represent the enthralling powers of the Masque, she may use her Pavane of Slaanesh three times in her Shooting phases.

EPIDEMIUS
THE TALLYMAN OF NURGLE

The task of cataloguing the potency of the Plaguelord's many and splendid diseases falls to Epidemius, the Lord of Decay's chosen Tallyman, one of the seven Proctors of Pestilence who preside over the Plaguebearers. Borne aloft on a rotten palanquin, Epidemius moves amongst the Daemons of Nurgle making note of all the varied afflictions and poxes unleashed into the universe. It is a never-ending task, for Nurgle is constantly creative and his anarchic hordes are ever keen to spread new and wonderful diseases.

Epidemius' Nurglings act as assistants, secreting ink for his quill, growing parchment-like strips of skin from their backs for their master to tear free, and counting upon a great death's head abacus that grows from the planks of the palanquin. The Nurglings also serve as guards for the Tallyman and swarm around any foe that approaches too closely. Unlike the usual babble and giggling that accompanies most Nurglings, Epidemius' brood are silent. They understand the importance of Epidemius' task and suffer his ire when an ill-timed titter or belch breaks his concentration. Only the slimy squelching of the Nurglings' progress and the gnawing scratch of Epidemius' quill break this sacred quietude.

In battle, Epidemius surveys the spread of filth and decay, taking note of every bubo, pustule and sore. Even as he writes, Father Nurgle becomes aware of Epidemius' learnings, distilling the information for future experiments and brews. If Epidemius were ever to make an error or an untimely observation, Nurgle's displeasure would be dire indeed and for this reason, Epidemius focuses wholly on his task even in the midst of desperate battle. Guided by his plaguesense, Epidemius follows the filthy spoor of his master's work through both the Daemon and mortal realms, seeking out new strands of virus, fresh species of bacteria and innovative symptoms of contagion.

	WS	BS	S	T	W	I	A	Ld	Sv
Epidemius	4	3	4	5	3	3	3	10	5+

Unit Type:
Infantry.

Daemonic Gifts:
Cloud of Flies, Plaguesword, Aura of Decay.

Special Rules:
Daemon, Slow & Purposeful, Feel no Pain, Independent Character.

The Tally of Pestilence: Whilst Epidemius is on the table, keep a count of all models killed by followers of Nurgle (i.e. any Daemon of Nurgle, or model with the Mark of Nurgle, both friends and enemies) anywhere on the table. At the start of each of your turns, consult the table below to determine the effect of the Tally of Pestilence. From the beginning of that turn, and as long as Epidemius is on the table, these cumulative bonuses affect all followers of Nurgle (friend and foe!).

Casualties	Effect
1-4	None
5-9	All Plagueswords, now wound on 3+
10-14	All followers of Nurgle have Noxious Touch
15-19	If a follower of Nurgle has Feel no Pain, it now saves on 3+
20+	All attacks from followers of Nurgle ignore armour saves!

THE BLUE SCRIBES
LIBRARIANS OF TZEENTCH

There was a time when Tzeentch ruled supreme over the other Gods of Chaos, his powers vastly superior than those of any of the Four (or so maintain his followers). In their envy and arrogance, the other gods set aside their differences and joined forces to overthrow the Grand Sorcerer. The entire universe was devastated in the cataclysmic conflict that followed. During the final battle, fearing that the combined armies of the other three Powers would eventually defeat him and take his crystal staff, symbol of his dominion and mightiest tool of power, Tzeentch opted for a more cautious tactic. The Great Schemer yielded, breaking his own crystal staff as a token of surrender. With a great sorcerous explosion, the staff shattered and its uncountable shards were flung to every corner of space and time, irremediably lost. This way Tzeentch made sure that nobody could wield as much power as he once did. Each shard of Tzeentch's crystal staff took the form of a different spell, a tiny fragment of his ultimate control over change. This event coincides with the birth of magic in the universe – for what is magic if not mastery over change!

After his defeat, Tzeentch created his Blue Scribes, P'tarix and Xirat'p in the shape of two Blue Horrors. He tasked them with the mission of travelling through the many dimensions of reality to find and record every known spell, eventually retrieving every single shard of his staff. Tzeentch has given his Scribes one of his flying Discs, both for speed and to carry the huge amount of parchment and ink that the two need for their task.

Not by chance has Tzeentch chosen two lowly Blue Horrors for such an important task. The Great Schemer, as always, was wary of what a Lord of Change or another craftier Daemon could do if it ever gained such a terrible power. With their limited intelligence, and being eternally in conflict with one another like all Blue Horrors, P'tarix and Xirat'p will never constitute a problem for their master.

Since then the Blue Scribes have appeared in the remotest corner of the galaxy, always searching for lost grimoires to copy and for skilled sorcerers to interrogate. Their peregrinations often lead them to the many battlefields of both the Warp and real space, where the two invariably end up helping the side Tzeentch wishes to win, whilst cataloguing all of the incantations used in the conflict by both sides. The two unleash a devastating magical barrage upon the enemy, reading from the huge collection of scrolls and grimoires they have collected performing their task through the centuries, while at the same time endlessly arguing about which spell to use next. If the two were ever to accomplish their mission, Tzeentch would regain his supremacy and once more rule over all creation.

	WS	BS	S	T	W	I	A	Ld	Sv
The Blue Scribes	2	4	3	3	2	4	3	10	4+

Unit Type:
Jump Infantry.

Daemonic Gifts:
We are Legion, Master of Sorcery, Bolt of Tzeentch, Boon of Mutation, Daemonic Gaze, Breath of Chaos, Pavane of Slaanesh, Aura of Decay, Warpfire.

Special Rules:
Daemon, Independent Character.

Watch this! The endless arguments of the Blue Scribes often result in petty squabbles about the best way to cast a spell, making them somehow unreliable... In their Shooting phase, before using their second ranged attack, roll a dice. On a 4-6 they proceed as normal. On a 1-3 they will use once again the same power they have just used.

THE CHANGELING
THE TRICKSTER OF TZEENTCH

The Changeling is unique amongst the Daemons of Tzeentch. The Great Deceiver has gifted his pet with the supernatural ability to assume the shape of any other creature with unfailing precision. So many times has the Changeling altered his appearance that even he has forgotten what his original shape was. Only the Great Schemer remembers it, and he keeps the secret for himself, for it gives him control of the Changeling.

The Changeling's powers, coupled with the immense knowledge that his Lord often grants him, make him the ultimate imitator. Many lords throughout the galaxy have made unusual and disastrous decisions, only to later deny they were even there; on many battlefields a great hero has fought an opponent that was his mirror-image, his comrades unable to tell the difference between the two until it was too late.

The Changeling is often busy behind enemy lines, sowing mistrust and confusion, which is his speciality. When he is not being used by Tzeentch as his trump card in the Great Game, the Changeling entertains himself by roaming the galaxy and the Warp alike to play devastating practical jokes upon the unwary.

On one occasion he took the shape of a Keeper of Secrets and answered the summoning of an Imperial commander whose vast palace was besieged by the vengeful Dark Angels Space Marines. The Changeling traded the souls of the desperate man's daughters for a 'powerful artefact', which in the fool's own words "would put an end to the siege". The moment the commander activated the strange device, the shadowy forms of several Deathwing Terminator squads materialised around him, locking onto the device he was holding in his hands – the teleport homer the Changeling had stolen from the Master of the Ravenwing's jetbike. The siege was indeed soon over.

	WS	BS	S	T	W	I	A	Ld	Sv
Changeling	2	3	3	3	1	3	1	10	4+

Unit Type:
Infantry. The Changeling is always fielded with a unit of Horrors, picked as a normal Troops choice. The Changeling is simply an upgrade character for this unit.

Special Rules:
Daemon.

Glamour of Tzeentch: The Changeling has a unique mind-bending power, which allows him to blur the perceptions of the enemy, making them see their own comrades as the most hideous of Daemons.

This power can be used in the enemy Shooting phase. Pick any enemy unit that is visible to the Changeling and is about to fire. If the unit is found to be within 24" of the Changeling, it is affected by his mind-altering mirage.

The unit may choose to hold its fire, and just stand around confused in this Shooting phase without moving. It may instead choose to open fire anyway, trying to see through the Glamour. In this case, the unit must take a Leadership test (vehicles are affected too, but count as Ld 10). If the test is passed, the unit sees through the Glamour and may fire as normal.

If the test is failed, the unit must immediately fire all of its weapons (no holding back!) against a friendly unit, chosen by the Changeling among any of the enemies he can see. If the Changeling cannot see a second enemy unit, the enemy which failed the test will simply stand around confused, as described above.

Daemonic Gifts:
Warpfire.

KARANAK
HOUND OF VENGEANCE

For those that incur the wrath of Khorne – mortal and Daemon alike – there is but one fate. Those who insult the Raging God's pride, warriors that break Khorne's creed, cowards that refuse to shed blood, Khorne's anger reaches them all. From one end of the multiverse to the other, across space and time, Karanak is the incarnation of Khorne's vengeance. Relentless, vicious and single-minded, Karanak hunts his prey across the warped daemon realms, through the depths of space, across swirling gas clouds and blazing supernovae. No army can defend against him, no wall can bar his path.

When not hunting, Karanak prowls the shadows of the Blood God's throne room. Karanak is ever-vigilant, for he has three heads and while one feeds on the bones of Khorne's sacrifices, the other two keep watch. None pass into Khorne's throne chamber save with the leave of this watchful guardian. Sometimes an unwary Bloodletter strays too close and Karanak pounces. It is a brutal end signalled by the snap of vertebrae, the spattering of blood and a chorus of chilling snarls.

As Khorne's ire rises, Karanak ceases his feeding and lopes to his master's side. With a roar, Khorne unleashes Karanak. The great hound of Khorne lifts his three heads, nostrils flaring as he catches the scent of his prey. He paces to and fro, growling and snarling as each head in turn savours a portion of the spoor. Each head can track Karanak's quarry in a different fashion. The first head follows the trail through space. The second tracks the scent through time. The third head, the most dangerous, senses the quarry through his thoughts, scenting their innermost feelings through dreamscapes and delusions. The third head guarantees that no prey eludes Karanak; those with wit and skill can avoid temporal detection, but no man outruns his own mind.

Once Karanak has fixed upon the odour of his victim, the Hound of Vengeance lopes forth on his hunt. Gathering pace as the trail grows stronger, Karanak bounds from realm to realm, flashing across insubstantial landscapes of nightmare, leaping from star to star. His growls echo in the dreams and waking thoughts of his target and his prey is overwhelmed by the foreshadow of approaching doom. Karanak's howls resound across space and time, drawing other Flesh Hounds to the chase. As the pursuit covers leagues and light years, a pack of slavering beasts forms around Karanak, hungry for the kill. Their howls join the roars of their leader as they approach their prey. In a frenzy of fangs and blood, Karanak and his daemonpack strike, tearing through anything in their path. Their quarry is quickly cornered and Karanak strikes, tearing hunks of flesh, eviscerating and dismembering with his metallic claws. It ends in moments. With the flopping, shredded remains of his victim clasped tightly in all three jaws, Karanak hurtles back to Khorne's throne room to present this gift to his master.

There, a pleased Blood God invariably adds the skull to the ever-growing pile upon which his throne sits.

	WS	BS	S	T	W	I	A	Ld	Sv
Karanak	5	0	5	4	1	4	3	10	5+

Unit Type:
Beasts. Karanak is always fielded with a unit of Flesh Hounds, picked as a normal Elites choice. Karanak is simply an upgrade character for this unit.

Daemonic Gifts:
Blessing of the Blood God, Fury of Khorne, Instrument of Chaos.

Special Rules:
Daemon, Furious Charge.

Prey of the Blood God: While Karanak is alive, the entire unit benefits from the Move Through Cover rule.

THE INFERNAL HOST

It's almost time to unleash your daemonic horde upon the weak mortal fools that dare oppose you. Firstly, here's a few tips on how to collect your force.

No other army fights quite like the Chaos Daemons. They appear out of nowhere, they are absolutely lethal in close assault, and are led by some of the most powerful individuals in the Warhammer 40,000 universe. With a bit of practice and some careful planning, you will have victory in your clawed grasp before your opponent knows what has hit him.

THE FULL GLORY OF CHAOS

From a gaming perspective, it makes a lot of sense to field as many types of Daemon as possible. Any army with so many different kinds of unit allows you far greater tactical flexibility. Each of the Daemon units tends to excel in a certain battlefield role, and when they work in conjunction with one another they can be unstoppable.

WARP BLEED

One of the most important decisions you can make when playing Daemons is how to divide your units before rolling for Daemonic Assault. Keep in mind that Daemons of Nurgle are an excellent choice for your first wave, as they can take an awesome amount of punishment and survive. Tzeentchian Daemons also come in very useful in the first wave, because their devastating ranged attacks can cripple or eliminate key enemy squads before your opponent can strike back. You should therefore make sure that you have at least one unit of either of these in your first wave, by placing at least one such unit in both groups. It is also a good idea to ensure that your first-wave will have at least one Chaos Icon, once again by putting at least one Icon in both groups, so that you can be assured that your reserves will enter play where you want them to.

The reserves should ideally include assault specialists such as Daemons of Khorne and Slaanesh; if an icon from your first wave has entered play close to the enemy, your assault specialists will often be able to get straight into combat without delay.

THE DAEMON LORDS

One of the greatest things about playing Chaos Daemons is the chance to field truly large and terrifying monsters. Greater Daemons are capable of laying waste to anything they can catch; the Bloodthirster in particular is especially feared. Imagine the look on your opponent's face when he sees that he has to contend with not one but two of these winged killing machines!

The Chaos Daemons army list also has some of the best value HQ choices in the game in the form of Daemonic Heralds. They still pack a punch, though, and as you can take up to four Heralds in your army they can really bolster the inherent skills of your rank-and-file Daemon packs whilst leaving you plenty of points for the more exotic units in your army.

MARKING THE BEAST

When painting your Daemons, one thing you may want to bear in mind is that sometimes your units will become intermingled – for instance in a close combat involving several Daemon units. For a conventional army it is easy enough to tell one unit from another because of squad markings or wargear, but Daemons are anything but conventional. As a result you need to be a little more imaginative with your squad markings. Perhaps you would like to field two or even three units of Bloodletters, for instance, and want to prevent the units from getting mixed up when they are butchering away. A great way to do this is to paint their tongues, swords, or hooves in a different colour for each unit. This works just as well for other Daemon units, just pick out a detail such as armour, claws, eyes, or pseudopods in a different colour.

THE ARMIES OF THE GODS

Some players will tend to gravitate towards a particular Chaos power, and field an army mostly, if not completely, comprised of troops that belong to that deity. Perhaps you like the no-holds-barred violence of a Khorne army, or the pustulent resilience of a Nurgle host! Because each Chaos power has several units that revere one god above all, this is a completely viable choice. Though it may cut down your tactical options somewhat, it does make for an extremely striking army, sure to be the envy (or terror) of your gaming companions. The best way to decide is to buy the models that appeal to you the most, and go from there!

No.	Model / Unit	Pts	Total	Choice
1	THE MASQUE	100	100	HQ
1	EPIDEMIUS	110	110	HQ
1	LORD OF CHANGE	240		HQ
	We are Legion	40	280	HQ
10	BLOODLETTERS	160		Troops
	All options	40	200	Troops
10	PLAGUEBEARRERS	150		Troops
	All options	35	185	Troops
10	HORRORS	170		Troops
	Bolt of Tzeentch	25	195	Troops
10	DAEMONETTES	140		Troops
	All options	35	175	Troops
3	NURGLINGS	39	39	Troops
5	FLAMERS	175	175	Elites
1	FIEND	30		Elites
	Unholy Might	10	40	Elites
1	BEAST	35	35	Elites
4	SCREAMERS	64	64	Fast Attack
6	FURIES	90	90	Fast Attack
1	SOUL GRINDER	135		Heavy Support
	Phlegm	25	160	Heavy Support
1	DAEMON PRINCE	80		Heavy Support
	Unholy Might	20		Heavy Support
	Daemonic Gaze	20		Heavy Support
	Iron Hide	30	150	Heavy Support
	TOTAL		**1998**	

This Daemon force is a majestic testament to Chaos in all its glory (2000 points, see its detailed army list in the box opposite). With so many different types of unit, it is very flexible and capable to take on any enemy.

This Cohort of Khorne Daemons (1500 points) is a lethal army that specialises in close combat. What it lacks in subtlety it more than makes up for in sheer killing power.

GREATER DAEMONS

▲ Rage incarnate!!

▲ The skulls of the worthiest foes.

▲ Bloodthirster:
Greater Daemon of Khorne

▲ Daemon weapons are always adorned with arcane glyphs.

▲ Many are the daemonic visages of the Keeper of Secrets.

▲ Keeper of Secrets:
Greater Daemon of Slaanesh

GREATER DAEMONS

▲ A powerful Daemon is bound within this staff

▲ Lord of Change:
Greater Daemon of Tzeentch

▲ Great Unclean One:
Greater Daemon of Nurgle

▲ Nurglings spawn from a Great Unclean One's rotten flesh...

▲ ...and then follow him around gleefully.

BLOODLETTERS OF KHORNE

▲ Bloodletter carrying an Instrument of Chaos

▲ A champion among Bloodletters, gifted with Fury of Khorne

▲ Bloodletter carrying an Icon of Chaos

Red is the colour of blood, slaughter and rage, and this is reflected in the many hues of the Bloodletters of Khorne.

▲ The Cloak of Skulls

▲ Skulltaker: The Champion of Khorne

► Blood and skulls always abound on the battle standards of the legions of Khorne.

▲ The legendary Hellblades are mighty tools of destruction, as sharp as Khorne's claws and still burning with the fires of the forge.

These Bloodletters were painted by John Blanche during his arcane studies on daemonic traits and anatomy. They differ from the ones painted by our 'Eavy Metal team and offer a great example of how you can personalise your own Daemon army.

DAEMONETTES OF SLAANESH

▲ Daemonette playing an Instrument of Chaos.

▲ The leaders among the Daemonettes can trasnfix a mortal with a single glance.

▲ Daemonette carrying an Icon of Chaos.

▲ Various hues of pink and purple, and contrasting gloss black, are among the favourite colours of the Lord of Excess and his Daemonic minions.

▲ The Masque of Slaanesh

▲ Daemonettes often decorate their skin, hair and claws with vivid colours and ornaments.

Daemonettes of Slaanesh charge into battle supported by Screamers of Tzeentch.

PLAGUEBEARERS OF NURGLE

▲ Epidemius, first among the Heralds of Nurgle.

▲ The many tools of the Tallyman of Nurgle

▲ Plaguebearer with an Instrument of Chaos

▲ A champion Plaguebearer gifted with Noxious Touch

▲ Plaguebearer with an Icon of Chaos.

All Plaguebearers have a single eye and a single horn, but are otherwise all the colours of rot and pus.

DAEMONS OF TZEENTCH

▲ The ever-flowing anatomy of the Flamers of Tzeentch is in itself an assault on the mortal mind.

Pink Horrors and Flamers prepare to unleash the Warpfire of Tzeentch against their enemy.

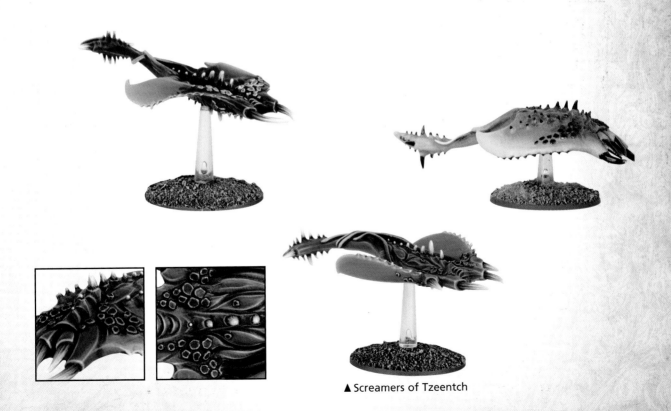

▲ Screamers of Tzeentch

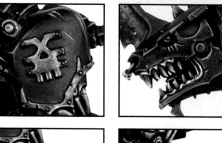

▲ An unstoppable Bloodcrusher of Khorne.

▲ Juggernauts are part Daemon, part machine.

▲ A Herald of Khorne on a mighty Juggernaut

FLESH HOUNDS OF KHORNE

The Flesh Hounds of Khorne bear collars and other ornaments marking them as servants of the Blood God.

Karanak leads a pack of Flesh Hounds to hunt down the enemies of his great Master.

FIENDS OF SLAANESH

▲ The Fiends of Slaanesh change colour according to the mood and whimsical aesthetic sense of the Dark Prince.

BEASTS OF NURGLE

▲ Beasts of Nurgle slither across the battlefield in search of new 'friends', leaving a foul slime trail behind them.

NURGLINGS

▲ A single Nurgling can be dangerous, but in their vast swarms they can become the most terrifying of plagues.

SOUL GRINDERS

▲ Harvester guns are used to mow down enemy infantry.

▲ This Soul Grinder's colours reveal it was originally
a Daemon of Khorne.

The Daemonic cohorts of Aradavak the Faithful ravage a mortal world.

As the power of Nurgle waxes, his Daemons emerge from the Warp to spread contagion through the galaxy.

DAEMONIC GIFTS

Many Daemons are given mighty weapons, great daemonic mounts and supernatural powers by their patron god. The following pages include Gifts of Chaos, Gifts of Khorne, Gifts of Tzeentch, Gifts of Slaanesh, Gifts of Nurgle, Marks of Chaos and Daemonic Steeds, all of which are equivalent to the weapons and other wargear used by mere mortals (note that these attacks are not psychic powers).

GIFTS OF CHAOS

BOON OF MUTATION
The Daemon may open a small conduit to the Immaterium, exposing the victim to the touch of the raw stuff of the Warp for a second. This often causes uncontrollable, lethal mutation in a mortal, at times turning the victim into a many-armed monstrosity.

Boon of Mutation is a ranged weapon, but the Daemon may be in close combat at the time it uses it, as may the target. Pick any one enemy model (no line of sight required) and roll to hit. If a hit is scored and the target is found to be within 6" of the Daemon, the target must immediately take a Toughness test. If the test is failed, the target is transformed into a shapeless blob of flesh and is removed as a casualty. Note that, as no wounds are taken, no saves apply! Models without a Toughness characteristic cannot be affected.

If the player using this Gift has a Chaos Spawn model available, he may replace the victim with a Spawn. If the model was in base contact with any models, move it so that it is 1" away from them. The Spawn is not a Daemon, but is a normal unit under the control of the player that used the Gift, with the profile and rules given below. The new Spawn may do nothing for the rest of the turn when it is created. If killed, it is worth 40 Victory points.

	WS	BS	S	T	W	I	A	Ld	Sv
Chaos Spawn	3	0	5	5	3	3	D6	10	-

Unit Type: Beasts

Special Rules: Fearless, Slow & Purposeful, Random Attacks (see Beast of Nurgle entry)

Mindless: Must always move as far as possible towards the closest enemy, must always try to assault the closest enemy, never counts as a scoring unit.

BREATH OF CHAOS
The Daemon can exhale a cloud of toxic gas or a cloud of mutagenic vapours against which no fortification is proof. Breath of Chaos is a template weapon. Any models fully or partially under the template suffer one wound on a D6 roll of 4+, with no Armour or Cover saves allowed! Vehicles touched by the template suffer a glancing hit on a D6 roll of 4+.

CHAOS ICON
An icon to the Dark Gods shines with the baleful energies of Chaos and is a perfect homing beacon for the Daemons as they break into reality.

When a friendly unit Deep Strikes within 6" of an Icon of Chaos it does not roll for scatter, provided that the icon was on the table from the beginning of the turn and has not arrived from Reserve in the same turn.

IRON HIDE
Some Daemon Princes were once mighty Lords from a Space Marine traitor Legion or renegade Chapter, and their bodies are still clad in the power armour of the Adeptus Astartes. Other Daemons may be blessed by their patron god with an impenetrable metal skin or a suit of Warp-forged armour.

Models with Iron Hide receive a 3+ Armour save.

DAEMONIC FLIGHT
Great pinioned wings or unfathomable arcane powers enable the Daemon to make great bounding leaps across the battlefield and swiftly race into close combat. Models with Daemonic Flight move like Jump Infantry, as described in the Warhammer 40,000 rulebook.

DAEMONIC GAZE
Rays of pure unholy energy burst from the eyes of the Daemon, incinerating its enemies. Daemonic Gaze is a ranged weapon with the following profile:

Range	Strength	AP	Type
24"	5	3	Assault 3

UNHOLY MIGHT
The Daemon has been granted exceptional strength, a true champion among its peers. The model has +1 Strength on its profile.

INSTRUMENT OF CHAOS
The Daemon carries a supernatural version of a warhorn, drum or other musical instrument, or perhaps it can emit a blood-chilling howl or a terrifying battle-cry. If the Daemon bearing this gift is involved in a fight which results in a draw, its side counts as having won by one wound. If both sides include an Instrument of Chaos, the result remains a draw.

GIFTS OF KHORNE

BLESSING OF THE BLOOD GOD

The Daemon wears a heavy studded collar or similar ornament as a symbol of Khorne's protection against magic. The Daemon has a 2+ Invulnerable save against wounds caused by psychic powers or force weapons.

DEATH STRIKE

As a champion of Khorne's subtler martial skills, the Daemon is armed with either a barbed whip, one of the infamous flaming brass skulls, or some other kind of devilry that extends its lethal reach. These are all ranged weapons with the following profile:

Range	Strength	AP	Type
12"	7	2	Assault 1

FURY OF KHORNE

The Daemon has been imbued with the distilled rage of his Master. The close combat attacks of a model gifted with the Fury of Khorne gain the Rending special rule.

HELLBLADE

Serrated swords forged in the fury of the Blood God, Hellblades are amongst the best cutting weapons in the universe. Hellblades are power weapons, as described in the Warhammer 40,000 rulebook.

GIFTS OF TZEENTCH

BOLT OF TZEENTCH

A solid beam of multi-coloured light strikes out of the Daemon's fingers and annihilates anything it touches, melting metals and vapourising flesh.

Bolt of Tzeentch is a ranged weapon with the following profile:

Range	Strength	AP	Type
24"	8	1	Assault 1

MASTER OF SORCERY

The Daemon has unparalleled magical knowledge, a true master of the arcane arts.

The model can use one extra ranged weapon in its Shooting phases (but not the same one twice, as normal).

SOUL DEVOURER

The Daemon can reach into an enemy's body, wrench out its soul and devour it. The Daemon counts as armed with a power weapon. In addition, if a model suffers any unsaved wounds from the Daemon's close combat attacks, it must immediately take a Leadership test for each wound suffered (on its own Leadership value, the model cannot use another model's Ld for this test). If any of these tests are failed, the victim suffers instant death.

WARPFIRE

The Daemon can summon and cast flaming, iridescent projectiles towards the enemy.

The Warpfire gift is a ranged weapon with the profile shown below:

Range	Strength	AP	Type
18"	4	4	Assault 3

WE ARE LEGION

The Daemon is host to many tortured souls, and different limbs, heads, eyes and leering faces continuously appear and vanish on every part of its ever-mutating body.

During the Shooting phase, the Daemon does not have to target all of its ranged weapons against the same target. Instead, it may fire any of its weapons at a different target (declare all targets before rolling to hit). It can then choose to assault any of the enemies it has fired against.

If the Daemon is an Independent Character and joins a unit, it can choose different targets from its unit's. Note that the unit is not affected by the shooting of the character in regards to which enemy they can assault in the ensuing Assault phase.

GIFTS OF SLAANESH

AURA OF ACQUIESCENCE
The Daemon is surrounded by a mind-altering aura that befuddles the enemy dramatically slowing their reactions when it matters the most.

Models with this Gift count as equipped with both assault grenades and defensive grenades (but receive no Strength bonus in close combat against vehicles).

PAVANE OF SLAANESH
The Daemon can emit an alluring song, forcing any who hear it into an ecstatic and enraptured dance.

The Pavane of Slaanesh is a ranged weapon with a range of 18". Roll to hit as normal. If the target unit is hit, it will immediately begin to dance to the tune of the Lord of Excess – the firer can immediately move the target unit up to D6". This movement follows the same rules as a normal move, except that it is not slowed by difficult terrain. So, for example, Dangerous Terrain tests are taken as normal, victims may not be moved off the table, out of combat, into impassable terrain or to within 1" of enemy models, and so on. An enemy unit may only be moved by this Gift once per turn, successive hits have no effect. The Pavane has no effect on vehicles other than Walkers, which are affected as normal (as they can dance!).

RENDING CLAWS
The barbed pincers of the many Daemons of Slaanesh are capable of lopping limbs off their opponents with delectable precision.

Rending Claws are a pair of close combat rending weapons, as described in the Warhammer 40,000 rulebook (the bonus attack is always included in the Daemon's profile).

SOPORIFIC MUSK
Enemies close to the Daemon find their minds confused, and their limbs heavy and slow.

The Daemon has the Hit & Run special rule.

TRANSFIXING GAZE
Transfixed by the magical gaze of the Daemon, the enemy cannot bring themselves to strike.

The player may force one model in base contact with the Daemon to lose an Attack in close combat.

GIFTS OF NURGLE

AURA OF DECAY
The sheer presence of the Daemon can strike down enemy warriors with an invisible curse of death. Aura of Decay is a ranged weapon, but the Daemon may be in close combat at the time it uses it, as may the targets. When used, all enemy models within 6" of the Daemon automatically suffer a Strength 2 hit with AP- (roll to wound as normal).

CLOUD OF FLIES
A swarm of flies envelopes the Daemon, distracting the enemy by flying into eyes, ears and mouths, and crawling under armour and clothing. Models with this Gift count as equipped with both assault grenades and defensive grenades (but receive no Strength bonus in close combat against vehicles).

NOXIOUS TOUCH
The Daemon and its weapons are covered in the most lethal toxic substance, instantly infecting any flesh it touches. The Daemon's close combat attacks are poisoned, wounding on a 2+, as described in the Warhammer 40,000 rulebook.

PLAGUESWORD
This gift from Father Nurgle is nothing more than an old rusted blade, but one that constantly secretes a lethal poisonous slime. Plague Swords are poisoned close combat weapons that wound all opponents on a 4+, as described in the Warhammer 40,000 rulebook.

> "Steel yourselves battle-brothers.
> The enemy approaches, I can feel them.
> They are all around us.
> And inside our very hearts.
>
> Only the Emperor can protect us now."
>
> *Librarian Azeroth at the Fall of Stygia VI*

DAEMONIC STEEDS

JUGGERNAUT OF KHORNE

This Daemonic Steed confers +1 Strength, +1 Toughness, +1 Wound, +1 Attack and the Iron Hide gift to the rider. A Khorne Herald's modified profile will then be as follows:

	WS	BS	S	T	W	I	A	Ld	Sv
Herald on Juggernaut	6	3	5	5	3	5	4	10	5+

CHARIOT OF KHORNE

In rare occasions, a Herald of Khorne who has distinguished himself with great deeds in the eyes of the Blood God is granted the boon of riding into battle on a great war-chariot. Pulled by a Juggernaut, this Daemonic Steed confers +1 Strength, +1 Toughness, +2 Wounds, +1 Attack and and the Iron Hide gift to the rider. In addition, the rider loses the Independent Character rule. A Khorne Herald's modified profile will then be as follows:

	WS	BS	S	T	W	I	A	Ld	Sv
Chariot of Khorne	6	3	5	5	4	5	4	10	5+

MOUNT OF SLAANESH

This Daemonic Steed confers +1 Attack to the Herald and changes its unit type from Infantry to Cavalry. Its modified profile will then be as follows:

	WS	BS	S	T	W	I	A	Ld	Sv
Herald on Mount of Slaanesh	5	3	3	3	2	7	5	10	5+

CHARIOT OF SLAANESH

The most gifted among the Handmaidens of the Lord of Excess are rewarded by their Master with a sleek chariot. Pulled by two Mounts of Slaanesh, this Daemonic Steed confers +2 Attacks, +1 Toughness, +3 Wounds and a 4+ armour save to the Herald, and changes its unit type from Infantry to Cavalry. In addition, the Herald replaces the Independent Character rule with the Furious Charge special rule. Its modified profile will then be as follows:

	WS	BS	S	T	W	I	A	Ld	Sv
Chariot of Slaanesh	5	3	3	4	5	7	6	10	5+

DISC OF TZEENTCH

This Daemonic Steed confers +1 Attack to the Herald and changes its unit type from Infantry to Jump Infantry. Its modified profile will then be as follows:

	WS	BS	S	T	W	I	A	Ld	Sv
Herald on Disc of Tzeentch	2	4	3	3	2	4	3	10	4+

CHARIOT OF TZEENTCH

The greatest artefact that Tzeentch can create for one of his Heralds is a supernatural flying chariot. Pulled by two Screamers, this Daemonic Steed confers +2 Attacks, +1 Toughness, +3 Wounds to the Herald and changes its unit type from Infantry to Jetbike. In addition, the Herald replaces the Independent Character rule with the Furious Charge special rule. Its modified profile will then be as follows:

	WS	BS	S	T	W	I	A	Ld	Sv
Chariot of Tzeentch	2	4	3	4	5	4	4	10	4+

PALANQUIN OF NURGLE

This Daemonic Steed confers +1 Attack and +1 Wound to the Herald. Its modified profile will then be as follows:

	WS	BS	S	T	W	I	A	Ld	Sv
Herald on Palanquin of Nurgle	4	3	4	5	3	3	3	10	5+

MARKS OF CHAOS

If a Daemon Prince is given the Mark of one of the Four Greater Powers of Chaos, it has been claimed by one of the Four as its own, and is given special powers in return. If a Daemon Prince model is given one of these Marks, its profile is modified as follows:

MARK OF KHORNE

5 Attacks (instead of 4).

MARK OF SLAANESH

Initiative 6 (instead of 5).

MARK OF NURGLE

Toughness 6 (instead of 5).

MARK OF TZEENTCH

4+ Invulnerable save (instead of 5+).

CHAOS DAEMONS ARMY LIST

The following army list enables you to field an army of Daemons and fight battles using the scenarios included in the Warhammer 40,000 rulebook.

USING THE ARMY LIST

The Chaos Daemons army list is split into five sections: HQ, Elites, Troops, Fast Attack and Heavy Support. All of the units in the army are placed into one of these depending upon their role on the battlefield. Each model is also given a points value, which varies depending on how effective that model is in battle.

Before you choose an army, you will need to agree with your opponent upon the type of game you are going to play and the maximum total number of points each of you will spend. Then you can proceed to pick your army using the Force Organisation Chart, as described in the paragraphs below.

THE FORCE ORGANISATION CHART

The army list is used in conjunction with the force organisation chart below, which is the one used for Standard Missions (see the Warhammer 40,000 rule book). The chart is split into five categories that correspond to the sections in the army list, and each category has one or more boxes. Each box indicates that you may make one choice from that section of the army list, while a dark-toned box indicates a compulsory selection – one that you must take.

If you and your opponent decide that you want to play a non-standard mission (for example one that you have designed yourselves), you are of course free to change the force organisation chart to suit the kind of game that you are about to play.

CHAOS DAEMONS FORCE ORGANISATION CHART

COMPULSORY	OPTIONAL
1 HQ	1 HQ
2 Troops	4 Troops
	3 Elites
	3 Fast Attack
	3 Heavy Support

ARMY LIST ENTRIES

Each entry in the army list represents a different unit. More information about the background and rules for the Daemons and their options can be found on pages 27-55, while information and examples of the Citadel miniatures you will need to represent them can be found on pages 56-72.

Each entry in the army list is split into several sections:

Unit Name: At the start of each entry you will find the name of the unit.

Models Cost: After the unit's name you will find the points cost of each model in the unit.

Unit Profile: The next line of the entry is the characteristics profile of the models in the unit. For more about characteristics, see the Warhammer 40,000 rulebook.

Unit Type: This line refers to the Warhammer 40,000 Unit Type rules chapter. A unit may be Infantry, Beast & Cavalry, Bikes, Jump Infantry, Artillery or Vehicle, and will be subject to a number of specific rules regarding its movement, shooting, assault, morale, etc.

Number/squad: This line shows the minimum number of models that you must include in the unit and the maximum that can be included.

For example, 5-20 means that the unit must include at least 5 models and cannot include more than 20.

Daemonic Gifts: This part details the Daemonic Gifts (upgrades) that models in the squad entry carry by default. The cost for all of these is included in the points cost of the models. It also includes optional upgrades in the shape of more Daemonic Gifts that can be bought for your models at an extra points cost.

Special Rules: Any special rules that apply to the unit are listed here. These special rules are explained in further detail in the Forces section. Some refer to the Universal Special Rules section of the Warhammer 40,000 rulebook.

For example, Daemonette units benefit from the 'Daemon' Special Rule, which is detailed in the Daemonic Forces section of this book, on page 27. They also have the 'Fleet' Special Rule, which can be found in the Warhammer 40,000 rulebook.

Options: This section lists all of the upgrades you may add to the unit if you wish to do so and their cost in points.

HQ

GREATER DAEMONS

These two pages present all of the Greater Daemons available to lead an army of Chaos Daemons.

Models that are marked as Unique under 'Number/squad' are individuals, and you may not include multiples of any of them in your army (you cannot field two Ku'gath or two Skulltakers, for example).

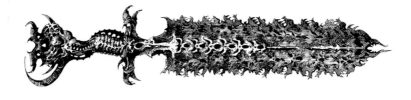

KU'GATH, THE PLAGUEFATHER COST: 300 POINTS   PAGE 48

	WS	BS	S	T	W	I	A	Ld	Sv
Ku'gath	6	4	6	6	6	2	5	10	4+

Unit Type:
Monstrous Creature

Number/squad:
Unique

Daemonic Gifts:
Cloud of Flies,
Noxious Touch,
Breath of Chaos,
Aura of Decay.

Special Rules:
Daemon, Feel No Pain,
Slow & Purposeful,
Necrotic Missiles,
Nurgling Infestation.

FATEWEAVER, ORACLE OF TZEENTCH COST: 333 POINTS   PAGE 49

	WS	BS	S	T	W	I	A	Ld	Sv
Fateweaver	4	5	5	5	3	4	2	9	3+

Unit Type:
Monstrous Creature

Number/squad:
Unique

Daemonic Gifts:
Soul Devourer,
Daemonic Flight,
Master of Sorcery,
We are Legion,
Breath of Chaos,
Daemonic Gaze,
Boon of Mutation,
Bolt of Tzeentch.

Special Rules:
Daemon,
Oracle of Eternity.

SKARBRAND, THE EXILED ONE COST: 300 POINTS   PAGE 47

	WS	BS	S	T	W	I	A	Ld	Sv
Skarbrand	10	0	8	6	4	5	6	10	4+

Unit Type:
Monstrous Creature

Number/squad:
Unique

Daemonic Gifts:
Iron Hide.

Special Rules:
Daemon, Fleet,
Furious Charge,
Rage Embodied,
Bellow of Endless Fury.

HQ

KEEPER OF SECRETS COST: 200 POINTS

	WS	BS	S	T	W	I	A	Ld	Sv
Keeper of Secrets	8	4	6	6	4	10	6	10	4+

Unit Type:
Monstrous Creature

Number/squad:
1

Daemonic Gifts:
Aura of Acquiescence.

Special Rules:
Daemon,
Fleet.

Options:
• May have any of the following:
- Transfixing Gaze .... +10 pts
- Soporific Musk .... +20 pts
- Pavane of Slaanesh .... +25 pts
- Daemonic Gaze .... +15 pts
- Unholy Might .... +15 pts
- Instrument of Chaos .... +5 pts

GREAT UNCLEAN ONE COST: 160 POINTS

PAGE 30

	WS	BS	S	T	W	I	A	Ld	Sv
Great Unclean One	6	4	6	6	5	2	4	10	4+

Unit Type:
Monstrous Creature

Number/squad:
1

Daemonic Gifts:
Noxious Touch.

Special Rules:
Daemon,
Feel No Pain,
Slow & Purposeful.

Options:
• May have any of the following:
- Cloud of Flies .... +5 pts
- Aura of Decay .... +20 pts
- Breath of Chaos ...... +30 pts
- Unholy Might .... +15 pts
- Instrument of Chaos .... +5 pts

BLOODTHIRSTER COST: 250 POINTS

PAGE 28

	WS	BS	S	T	W	I	A	Ld	Sv
Bloodthirster	10	4	7	6	4	5	5	10	4+

Unit Type:
Monstrous Creature

Number/squad:
1

Daemonic Gifts:
Iron Hide,
Daemonic Flight.

Special Rules:
Daemon,
Furious Charge.

Options:
• May have any of the following:
- Death Strike .... +20 pts
- Blessing of the
  Blood God .... +5 pts
- Unholy Might .... +20 pts
- Instrument of Chaos .... +5 pts

LORD OF CHANGE COST: 250 POINTS

PAGE 31

	WS	BS	S	T	W	I	A	Ld	Sv
Lord of Change	5	5	6	6	4	5	3	10	3+

Unit Type:
Monstrous Creature

Number/squad:
1

Daemonic Gifts:
Soul Devourer,
Daemonic Gaze,
Bolt of Tzeentch,
Daemonic Flight.

Special Rules:
Daemon.

Options:
• May have any of the following:
- We are Legion .... +40 pts
- Master of Sorcery ...... +10 pts
- Breath of Chaos .... +30 pts
- Boon of Mutation ..... +30 pts
- Instrument of Chaos .... +5 pts

ARMY LIST   79

HQ

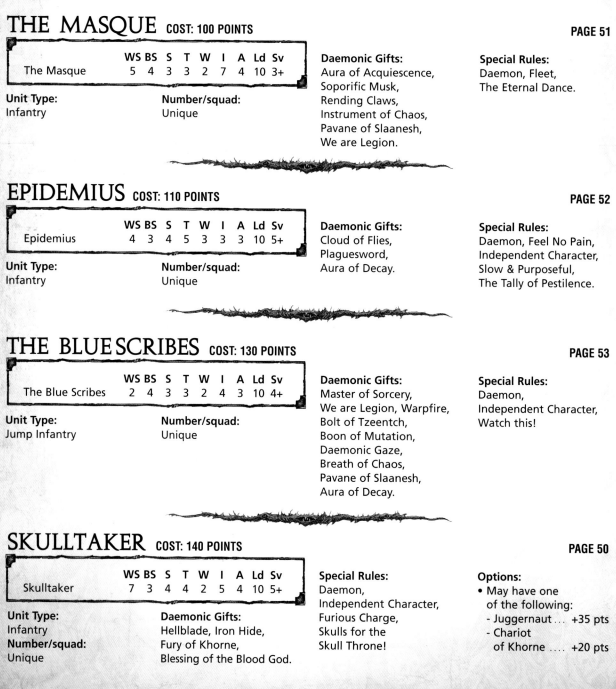

THE MASQUE COST: 100 POINTS

PAGE 51

	WS	BS	S	T	W	I	A	Ld	Sv
The Masque	5	4	3	3	2	7	4	10	3+

Unit Type:
Infantry

Number/squad:
Unique

Daemonic Gifts:
Aura of Acquiescence,
Soporific Musk,
Rending Claws,
Instrument of Chaos,
Pavane of Slaanesh,
We are Legion.

Special Rules:
Daemon, Fleet,
The Eternal Dance.

EPIDEMIUS COST: 110 POINTS

PAGE 52

	WS	BS	S	T	W	I	A	Ld	Sv
Epidemius	4	3	4	5	3	3	3	10	5+

Unit Type:
Infantry

Number/squad:
Unique

Daemonic Gifts:
Cloud of Flies,
Plaguesword,
Aura of Decay.

Special Rules:
Daemon, Feel No Pain,
Independent Character,
Slow & Purposeful,
The Tally of Pestilence.

THE BLUE SCRIBES COST: 130 POINTS

PAGE 53

	WS	BS	S	T	W	I	A	Ld	Sv
The Blue Scribes	2	4	3	3	2	4	3	10	4+

Unit Type:
Jump Infantry

Number/squad:
Unique

Daemonic Gifts:
Master of Sorcery,
We are Legion, Warpfire,
Bolt of Tzeentch,
Boon of Mutation,
Daemonic Gaze,
Breath of Chaos,
Pavane of Slaanesh,
Aura of Decay.

Special Rules:
Daemon,
Independent Character,
Watch this!

SKULLTAKER COST: 140 POINTS

PAGE 50

	WS	BS	S	T	W	I	A	Ld	Sv
Skulltaker	7	3	4	4	2	5	4	10	5+

Unit Type:
Infantry
Number/squad:
Unique

Daemonic Gifts:
Hellblade, Iron Hide,
Fury of Khorne,
Blessing of the Blood God.

Special Rules:
Daemon,
Independent Character,
Furious Charge,
Skulls for the
Skull Throne!

Options:
• May have one
of the following:
- Juggernaut ... +35 pts
- Chariot
of Khorne .... +20 pts

HQ

HERALD OF KHORNE   COST: 70 POINTS

PAGE 32

	WS	BS	S	T	W	I	A	Ld	Sv
Herald of Khorne	6	3	4	4	2	5	3	10	5+

Unit Type:
Infantry

Number/squad:
1

Daemonic Gifts:
Hellblade.

Special Rules:
Daemon,
Independent Character,
Furious Charge.

Options:
- May have one of the following:
  - Juggernaut .... +35 pts
  - Chariot of Khorne .... +15 pts
- May have three of the following:
  - Fury of Khorne .... +10 pts
  - Death Strike .... +15 pts
  - Blessing of the Blood God .... +5 pts
  - Iron Hide .... +15 pts
  - Chaos Icon .... +25 pts
  - Unholy Might .... +15 pts

HERALD OF TZEENTCH   COST: 50 POINTS

PAGE 35

	WS	BS	S	T	W	I	A	Ld	Sv
Herald of Tzeentch	2	4	3	3	2	4	2	10	4+

Unit Type:
Infantry

Number/squad:
1

Daemonic Gifts:
Daemonic Gaze.

Special Rules:
Daemon,
Independent Character.

Options:
- May have one of the following:
  - Disc of Tzeentch .... +15 pts
  - Chariot of Tzeentch .... +15 pts
- May have three of the following:
  - We are Legion .... +10 pts
  - Master of Sorcery .... +5 pts
  - Soul Devourer .... +20 pts
  - Bolt of Tzeentch .... +30 pts
  - Breath of Chaos .... +30 pts
  - Chaos Icon .... +25 pts
  - Boon of Mutation .... +30 pts

HERALD OF NURGLE   COST: 50 POINTS

PAGE 34

	WS	BS	S	T	W	I	A	Ld	Sv
Herald of Nurgle	4	3	4	5	2	3	2	10	5+

Unit Type:
Infantry

Number/squad:
1

Daemonic Gifts:
Plaguesword.

Special Rules:
Daemon, Feel No Pain,
Independent Character,
Slow & Purposeful.

Options:
- May ride a Palanquin of Nurgle .... +15 pts
- May have three of the following:
  - Noxious Touch .... +10 pts
  - Chaos Icon .... +25 pts
  - Cloud of Flies .... +5 pts
  - Aura of Decay .... +15 pts
  - Breath of Chaos .... +30 pts
  - Unholy Might .... +10 pts

HERALD OF SLAANESH   COST: 50 POINTS

PAGE 33

	WS	BS	S	T	W	I	A	Ld	Sv
Herald of Slaanesh	5	3	3	3	2	7	4	10	5+

Unit Type:
Infantry

Number/squad:
1

Daemonic Gifts:
Rending Claws,
Aura of Acquiescence.

Special Rules:
Daemon, Fleet,
Independent Character.

Options:
- May have one of the following:
  - Mount of Slaanesh .... +15 pts
  - Chariot of Slaanesh .... +15 pts
- May have three of the following:
  - Transfixing Gaze .... +5 pts
  - Soporific Musk .... +15 pts
  - Chaos Icon .... +25 pts
  - Pavane of Slaanesh .... +20 pts
  - Daemonic Gaze .... +15 pts
  - Unholy Might .... +10 pts

ELITES

FIENDS OF SLAANESH COST: 30 POINTS EACH

PAGE 37

	WS	BS	S	T	W	I	A	Ld	Sv
Fiend	4	0	5	4	2	5	5	10	5+

Unit Type:
Beasts

Number/squad:
1-6

Daemonic Gifts:
Soporific Musk,
Rending Claws.

Special Rules:
Daemon.

Options:
• Gift one model with:
  - Unholy Might ..... +10 pts

FLAMERS OF TZEENTCH COST: 35 POINTS EACH

PAGE 39

	WS	BS	S	T	W	I	A	Ld	Sv
Flamer	2	4	4	4	1	3	2	10	4+

Unit Type:
Jump Infantry

Number/squad:
3-12

Daemonic Gifts:
Warpfire,
Breath of Chaos.

Special Rules:
Daemon.

Options:
• Gift one model with:
  - Bolt of Tzeentch .. +30 pts

THE CAGED MAIDEN

The Eldar believe that their gods are dead, destroyed by Slaanesh when the Dark Prince awoke. Yet there is one myth upon a single craftworld that tells of how the maiden goddess Isha was not slain by the Prince of Pleasure. Instead, when Slaanesh claimed Isha as his own, Nurgle heard her cries for help and her anguish touched his leprous heart.

Isha was a goddess of fertility and healing, the embodiment of life, and mighty Nurgle wished for her to become his companion. Nurgle waged a long war against Slaanesh to wrest Isha from the Dark Prince's grasp and was eventually victorious.

Yet the adoration of a Chaos God is a strange thing, for Nurgle shows his affection in cruel ways. Nurgle keeps Isha within a rusted cage in the corner of his cauldron chamber. When the Plague God creates a particularly pleasing brew, he forces Isha to imbibe the putrid mixture, watching with building excitement for the symptoms of his latest contagion.

Though Isha can cure herself of the disease's ravages, the speed with which she is freed from its grip allows the Plaguelord to evaluate his creation's virulence. If Nurgle is pleased, he returns to his cauldron and empties its contents into a bottomless drain, the noxious liquid falling as rain upon one of the mortal worlds. If the concoction does not meet with Nurgle's approval, he gulps down the contents of the cauldron, vomits it back into the pot and starts afresh. While the Plaguefather is busy at his cauldron, Isha whispers to mortals, seeking to tell them the cures for the poxes she has tasted.

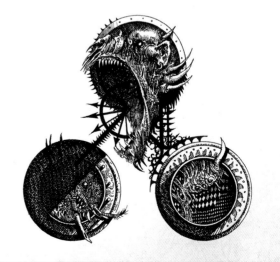

ELITES

BLOODCRUSHERS OF KHORNE COST: 40 POINTS EACH PAGE 40

	WS	BS	S	T	W	I	A	Ld	Sv
Bloodcrusher	5	0	5	5	2	4	3	10	5+

Unit Type:
Infantry

Number/squad:
1-8

Daemonic Gifts:
Hellblade,
Iron Hide.

Special Rules:
Daemon,
Furious Charge.

Options:
• Gift one model with:
  - Fury of Khorne .... +10 pts

• Gift another model with:
  - Chaos Icon .... +25 pts

• Gift another model with:
  - Instrument
    of Chaos .... +5 pts

BEASTS OF NURGLE COST: 35 POINTS EACH PAGE 38

	WS	BS	S	T	W	I	A	Ld	Sv
Beast	3	0	4	5	2	2	D6	10	5+

Unit Type:
Infantry

Number/squad:
1-7

Special Rules:
Daemon,
Random Poisoned
Attacks,
Feel No Pain,
Slow & Purposeful.

Options:
• Gift one model with:
  - Noxious Touch ..... +10 pts

THE CLEANSING OF THOTH

At the height of the Macharian Crusades, the Imperium's forces came upon the desert world of Thoth. This world could not be brought back to the fold of the Imperium, for its population had strayed too far from the Light of the Emperor, having turned to the worship of the powers of the Warp. Its twisted inhabitants could not be allowed to live, and so Lord Solar Macharius ordered them exterminated.

But the Witches of Thoth called upon the elemental spirits of the desert night, and brought about a worldwide daemonic incursion in a single night of blasphemy and sacrifice. The invading Imperial Guard were scattered as the skies boiled with witch fire, and the drop zones soon became killing fields strewn with blackened bones gnawed on by gibbering Daemons.

But one force did survive the massacre, and its leader, the celebrated Captain El'rahem, made contact with previously unknown tribesmen residing in the deep desert. These nomads were uncorrupted by Chaos, and bore a burning hatred for the witches that ruled their world. A natural leader, El'rahem united the tribes of the N'go, and led them in a war against the foul creatures swarming across the world. Though the tribes were almost wiped out in the savage conflict, El'rahem's armies were ultimately successful in defeating the forces of Chaos.

Yet for all the Guard and tribesmen's triumphs, Thoth was declared 'Amundi Heretica'. As El'rahem and his allies were evacuated, the world was virus bombed by sleek, black Inquisition execution ships. No living thing was left upon Thoth; no human souls remained to call forth the beasts of the Warp with unholy entreaties.

TROOPS

BLOODLETTERS OF KHORNE   COST: 16 POINTS EACH   PAGE 32

	WS	BS	S	T	W	I	A	Ld	Sv
Bloodletter	5	0	4	4	1	4	2	10	5+

Unit Type:
Infantry

Number/squad:
5-20

Daemonic Gifts:
Hellblade.

Special Rules:
Daemon,
Furious Charge.

Options:
• Gift one model with:
  - Fury of Khorne .... +10 pts

• Gift another model with:
  - Chaos Icon .... +25 pts

• Gift another model with:
  - Instrument
    of Chaos .... +5 pts

DAEMONETTES OF SLAANESH   COST: 14 POINTS EACH   PAGE 33

	WS	BS	S	T	W	I	A	Ld	Sv
Daemonette	4	0	3	3	1	6	3	10	5+

Unit Type:
Infantry

Number/squad:
5-20

Daemonic Gifts:
Rending Claws,
Aura of Acquiescence.

Special Rules:
Daemon,
Fleet.

Options:
• Gift one model with:
  - Transfixing Gaze .... +5 pts

• Gift another model with:
  - Chaos Icon .... +25 pts

• Gift another model with:
  - Instrument
    of Chaos .... +5 pts

PLAGUEBEARERS OF NURGLE   COST: 15 POINTS EACH   PAGE 34

	WS	BS	S	T	W	I	A	Ld	Sv
Plaguebearer	3	0	4	5	1	2	1	10	5+

Unit Type:
Infantry

Number/squad:
5-20

Daemonic Gifts:
Plaguesword.

Special Rules:
Daemon,
Slow & Purposeful,
Feel No Pain.

Options:
• Gift one model with:
  - Noxious Touch ..... +10 pts

• Gift another model with:
  - Chaos Icon .... +25 pts

• Gift another model with:
  - Instrument
    of Chaos .... +5 pts

TROOPS

PINK HORRORS OF TZEENTCH COST: 17 POINTS EACH PAGE 35

	WS	BS	S	T	W	I	A	Ld	Sv
Pink Horror	2	3	3	3	1	3	1	10	4+

Unit Type:
Infantry

Number/squad:
5-20

Daemonic Gifts:
Warpfire.

Special Rules:
Daemon.

Options:
• Gift one model with:
  - Bolt of
    Tzeentch .... +10 pts

• Gift another model with:
  - Chaos Icon ..... +25 pts

• Gift another model with:
  - Instrument
    of Chaos .... +5 pts

• Upgrade another model
  (once per army) to:
  - The Changeling . +5 pts

THE CHANGELING PAGE 54

	WS	BS	S	T	W	I	A	Ld	Sv
Changeling	2	3	3	3	1	3	1	10	4+

Unit Type:
Infantry

Number/squad:
Unique

Daemonic Gifts:
Warpfire.

Special Rules:
Daemon,
Glamour of Tzeentch.

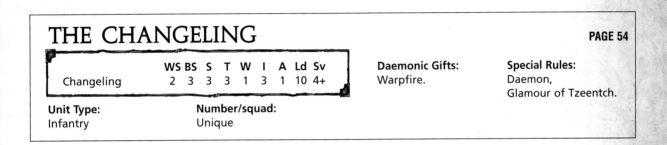

NURGLINGS COST: 13 POINTS PER BASE PAGE 42

	WS	BS	S	T	W	I	A	Ld	Sv
Nurglings	2	0	3	3	3	2	3	10	5+

Unit Type:
Infantry

Number/squad:
3-9

Special Rules:
Daemon, Swarm.

FAST ATTACK

FLESH HOUNDS OF KHORNE COST: 15 POINTS EACH

PAGE 36

	WS	BS	S	T	W	I	A	Ld	Sv
Flesh Hound	4	0	4	4	1	4	2	10	5+

Unit Type:
Beasts

Number/squad:
5-20

Daemonic Gifts:
Blessing of the Blood God.

Special Rules:
Daemon, Furious Charge.

Options:
- Gift one model with:
  - Fury of Khorne .... +10 pts

- Upgrade another model (once per army) to:
  - Karanak .... +35 pts

KARANAK, HOUND OF VENGEANCE

PAGE 55

	WS	BS	S	T	W	I	A	Ld	Sv
Karanak	5	0	5	4	1	4	3	10	5+

Unit Type:
Beasts

Number/squad:
Unique

Daemonic Gifts:
Fury of Khorne, Blessing of the Blood God, Instrument of Chaos.

Special Rules:
Daemon, Furious Charge, Prey of the Blood God.

SEEKERS OF SLAANESH COST: 17 POINTS EACH

PAGE 41

	WS	BS	S	T	W	I	A	Ld	Sv
Seeker	4	0	3	3	1	6	4	10	5+

Unit Type:
Cavalry

Number/squad:
5-20

Daemonic Gifts:
Rending Claws, Aura of Acquiescence.

Special Rules:
Daemon.

Options:
- Gift one model with:
  - Transfixing Gaze .... +5 pts

- Gift another model with:
  - Chaos Icon .... +25 pts

- Gift another model with:
  - Instrument of Chaos .... +5 pts

SCREAMERS OF TZEENTCH COST: 16 POINTS EACH

PAGE 43

	WS	BS	S	T	W	I	A	Ld	Sv
Screamers	3	0	4	4	1	3	1	10	4+

Unit Type:
Jetbikes

Number/squad:
3-12

Special Rules:
Daemon, Warp Jaws.

Options:
- Gift one model with:
  - Unholy Might .... +5 pts

FURIES OF CHAOS COST: 15 POINTS EACH

PAGE 46

	WS	BS	S	T	W	I	A	Ld	Sv
Fury	3	0	4	4	1	3	2	10	5+

Unit Type:
Jump Infantry

Number/squad:
5-20

Special Rules:
Daemon.

HEAVY SUPPORT

SOUL GRINDER OF CHAOS COST: 135 POINTS

PAGE 44

	Armour							
	WS	BS	S	F	S	R	I	A
Soul Grinder	3	3	6	13	13	11	3	4

Unit Type:
Vehicle (Walker)

Number/squad:
1

Special Rules:
Daemon, Fleet.

Wargear:
- Two Dreadnought close combat weapons (extra attack included in profile).
- One Harvester built into one of the close combat weapons.
- One Mawcannon ('Vomit' weapon profile only).

Options:
- Upgrade the Mawcannon to be able to use any of the following profiles:
  - Phlegm ....+25 pts
  - Tongue ....+25 pts

DAEMON PRINCE OF CHAOS COST: 80 POINTS

PAGE 46

	WS	BS	S	T	W	I	A	Ld	Sv
Daemon Prince	7	5	5	5	4	5	4	10	5+

Unit Type:
Monstrous Creature

Number/squad:
1

Special Rules:
Daemon.

Options:
- May have any of the following:
  - Daemonic Flight ....+60 pts
  - Iron Hide ....+30 pts
  - Instrument of Chaos ....+5 pts
  - Unholy Might ....+20 pts
- May have one of the following:
  - Mark of Khorne ....+15 pts
  - Mark of Slaanesh ....+10 pts
  - Mark of Nurgle ....+30 pts
  - Mark of Tzeentch ....+25 pts
- Models with the Mark of Tzeentch may have any of the following:
  - Master of Sorcery ....+10 pts
  - Soul Devourer ....+10 pts
  - Bolt of Tzeentch ....+35 pts
- Models with the Mark of Khorne may have any of the following:
  - Blessing of the Blood God .....+10 pts
  - Death Strike ....+20 pts
- Models with the Mark of Slaanesh may have any of the following:
  - Aura of Acquiescence ....+5 pts
  - Soporific Musk ....+20 pts
  - Transfixing gaze ....+10 pts
  - Pavane of Slaanesh ....+30 pts
- Models with the Mark of Nurgle may have any of the following:
  - Cloud of Flies ....+5 pts
  - Noxious Touch ....+10 pts
  - Aura of Decay ....+20 pts
- Models that do not have the Mark of Khorne may also have one of the following (models with the Mark of Tzeentch may have up to two):
  - Daemonic Gaze ....+20 pts
  - Breath of Chaos ....+30 pts
  - Boon of Mutation ....+30 pts

SUMMARY

	WS	BS	S	T	W	I	A	Ld	Sv	Page
Beast of Nurgle	3	0	4	5	2	2	D6	10	5+	38
Bloodletter of Khorne	5	0	4	4	1	4	2	10	5+	32
Bloodcrusher of Khorne	5	0	5	5	2	4	3	10	5+	40
Bloodthirster	10	4	7	6	4	5	5	10	4+	28
The Blue Scribes	2	4	3	3	2	4	3	10	4+	53
The Changeling	2	3	3	3	1	3	1	10	4+	54
Daemon Prince	7	5	5	5	4	5	4	10	5+	46
Daemonette of Slaanesh	4	0	3	3	1	6	3	10	5+	33
Epidemius	4	3	4	5	3	3	3	10	5+	52
Fateweaver	4	5	5	5	3	4	2	9	3+	49
Fiend of Slaanesh	4	0	5	4	2	5	5	10	5+	37
Flamer of Tzeentch	2	4	4	4	1	3	2	10	4+	39
Flesh Hound of Khorne	4	0	4	4	1	4	2	10	5+	36
Fury of Chaos	3	0	4	4	1	3	2	10	5+	46
Great Unclean One	6	4	6	6	5	2	4	10	4+	30
Herald of Khorne	6	3	4	4	2	5	3	10	5+	32

	WS	BS	S	T	W	I	A	Ld	Sv	Page
Herald of Nurgle	4	3	4	5	2	3	2	10	5+	34
Herald of Slaanesh	5	3	3	3	2	7	4	10	5+	33
Herald of Tzeentch	2	4	3	3	2	4	2	10	4+	35
Karanak	5	0	5	4	1	4	3	10	5+	55
Keeper of Secrets	8	4	6	6	4	10	6	10	4+	29
Ku'gath	6	4	6	6	6	2	5	10	4+	48
Lord of Change	5	5	6	6	4	5	3	10	3+	31
The Masque	5	4	3	3	2	7	4	10	3+	51
Nurglings	2	0	3	3	3	2	3	10	5+	42
Pink Horror of Tzeentch	2	3	3	3	1	3	1	10	4+	35
Plaguebearer of Nurgle	3	0	4	5	1	2	1	10	5+	34
Screamer of Tzeentch	3	0	4	4	1	3	1	10	4+	43
Seeker of Slaanesh	4	0	3	3	1	6	4	10	5+	41
Skarbrand	10	0	8	6	4	5	6	10	4+	47
Skulltaker	7	3	4	4	2	5	4	10	5+	50

Armour

	WS	BS	S	F	S	R	I	A		Page
Soul Grinder	3	3	6	13	13	11	3	4		44

Written by: Alessio Cavatore. **Additional text:** Gav Thorpe, Phil Kelly. **Cover art:** Adrian Smith.
Illustrations: John Blanche, Alex Boyd, Paul Dainton, Nuala Kinrade, Adrian Smith, Ian Miller & Robin Carey.
Graphic design: Pete Borlace. **Production Lead:** Tim Vincent. **Photography:** Stuart White & Ian Strickland. **Production:** Simon Burton, Chris Eggar, & Chris Ward.
Hobby material: Dave Andrews, Mark Jones & Chad Mierzwa. **Editing:** Talima Fox.
Miniatures design: Aly Morrison, Trish Morrison, Alex Hedstrom, Juan Diaz, Mike Anderson, Jes Goodwin, Mark Harrison & Brian Nelson.
'Eavy Metal: Pete Foley, Darren Latham, Neil Langdown, Neil Green, Keith Robertson, Kirsten Williams, Fil Dunn, Anja Wettergren.
Special thanks: Alan Merrett, Rick Priestley, Mat Ward, Jervis Johnson, Jeremy Vetock, Graham Davey.

PRODUCED BY GAMES WORKSHOP

UK
Games Workshop Ltd.,
Willow Rd, Lenton,
Nottingham,
NG7 2WS

US
Games Workshop Inc,
6721 Baymeadow Drive,
Glen Burnie,
Maryland, 21060-6401

CANADA
Games Workshop,
2679 Bristol Circle,
Unit 3, Oakville,
Ontario, L6H 6Z8

AUSTRALIA
Games Workshop,
23 Liverpool Street,
Ingleburn,
NSW 2565

NORTHERN EUROPE
Games Workshop Ltd.,
Willow Rd, Lenton,
Nottingham,
NG7 2WS